TOP 20
CODING INTERVIEW PROBLEMS
ASKED IN GOOGLE WITH SOLUTIONS

Algorithmic Approach

LIN QUAN

ISBN-13: 978-1495466571
ISBN-10: 1495466574

Preface

This book is written for helping people prepare for Google Coding Interview. It contains top 20 programming problems frequently asked @Google with detailed worked-out solutions both in pseudo-code and C++(and C++11).

It came out as a result of numerous requests received from coders across the Globe, primarily from Google aspirants. Author has a vast collection of algorithmic problems since 20 years including experience in preparing computer science students for participation in programming contests like TopCoder, ACM ICPC and others.

For suggestions, feedback and comments, the author can be contacted at : *lin.quan.20@gmail.com*

Lin Quan

List of Chapters

List of Chapters

List of Chapters

List of Chapters

List of Algorithms

List of Chapters

List of Programs

List of Programs

Chapter 1

Matching Nuts and Bolts Optimally

Problem 1 (*G. J. E. Rawlings*)

There is a bag full of n *nuts and* n *bolts, each of distinct sizes, such that there is one-to-one correspondence between the nuts and the bolts, i.e., for every nut, there is a bolt and vice verse. Nuts cannot be compared to nuts and bolts cannot be compared to bolts directly, but nuts can be compared to bolts by trying to fit one into the other. Design and implement an optimal algorithm for fitting all nuts to bolts. By optimal we mean to minimize the number of comparisons involved in the algorithm.*

Solution

1.1 Basic Analysis

The same problem can be posed to a computer scientist as follows:

Given two sets $B : \{b_1, \ldots, b_n\}$ and $N : \{n_1, \ldots, n_n\}$, where B is a set of n distinct real numbers (representing the sizes of the bolts) and N is a permutation of B, we wish to find efficiently the unique permutation $\sigma \in N_n$ so that $b_i = n_{\sigma(i)} \forall i$, based on queries of the form *compare b_i and n_j*. The answer to each such query is either

1. $b_i > n_j$ or
2. $b_i = n_j$ or
3. $b_i < n_j$

Since there are n! possibilities for σ, the obvious information theoretic lower bound shows that any bounded degree decision tree that solves the problem has depth at least $\log_3(n!)$.

Using Sterling's approximation :

$$\log_3(n!) \approx \theta(n \log_3 n)$$

Similar to comparison-based sorting, it can be analyzed using decision tree. Please note that we can model any algorithm for matching nuts and bolts as a decision tree.

The tree will be a *ternary tree*, since every comparison has *three* possible outcomes:

1. *less than,*
2. *equal, or*
3. *greater than*

The height of such a tree corresponds to the worst-case number of comparisons made by the algorithm it represents, which in turn is a lower bound on the running time of that algorithm. We therefore want a lower bound of $\Omega(n \log n)$ on the height, H, of any decision tree that solves nuts n bolts problem mentioned in earlier section.

To begin with, note that the number of leaves L in any ternary tree must satisfy $L \leq 3^H$. Next, consider the following class of inputs.

Let the input array of nuts N be fixed and consist of n nuts in increasing sorted order, and consider one potential input for every permutation of the bolts. In order to match the nuts and bolts, our algorithm must in this case essentially sort the array of bolts.

In our decision tree, if two different inputs of this type were mapped to the same leaf node, our algorithm would attempt to apply to both of these the same permutation of bolts with respect to nuts, and it follows that the algorithm could not compute a matching correctly for both of these inputs.

Therefore, we must map every one of these n! different inputs to a distinct leaf node, i.e.

$$L \geq n!$$
$$\implies 3^H \geq n!$$
$$\implies H \geq \log_3 n$$
$$\implies H = \Omega(n \log n)$$

Please note that base of logarithm doesn't matter in complexity, it is a kind of constant, so we will ignore this too.

In particular, at least $\Omega(n \log n)$ comparisons are needed. This is a lower bound for the expected number of comparisons in any randomized algorithm for the problem as well.

A simple modification of *Randomized Quicksort* shows that there are simple randomized algorithms whose expected number of comparisons (and running time) are $O(n \log n)$:

- pick a random bolt
- compare it to all the nuts
- find its matching nut, thus splitting the nuts into three parts:
    1. nuts smaller for the bolt
    2. nuts exactly fit with the bolt
    3. nuts bigger for the bolt
- compare the matching nut found above to rest of the remaining $n - 1$ bolts, thus splitting the bolts into three parts:
    1. bolts looser for the nut
    2. bolt exactly fit to the nut
    3. bolts tighter for the nut
- thus splitting the problem into two problems, one consisting of the nuts and bolts smaller than the matched pair and one consisting of the larger ones.

This pair of partitioning operations can easily implemented in $\Theta(n)$ time, and it leaves the nuts and bolts nicely partitioned so that the *pivot* nut and bolt are aligned with each-other and all other nuts and bolts are on the correct side of these pivots :

- smaller nuts and bolts precede the pivots, and
- larger nuts and bolts follow the pivots.

This algorithm then finishes by recursively applying itself to the subarrays to the left and right of the pivot position to match these remaining nuts and bolts. We can assume by induction on n that these recursive calls will properly match the remaining bolts.

To analyze the running time of this algorithm, we can use the same analysis as that of *randomized quicksort*. We are performing a partition operation in $\Theta(n)$ time that splits our problem into two subproblems whose sizes are randomly distributed exactly as would be the subproblems resulting from a partition in randomized quicksort. Therefore, applying the analysis from quicksort, the expected running time of our algorithm is $\Theta(n \log n)$.

This problem provides a striking example of how randomization can help simplify the task of algorithm design.

Rawlins[1] posed this problem as :

> We wish to sort a bag of n nuts and n bolts by size in the dark. We can compare the sizes of a nut and a bolt by attempting to screw one into the other. This operation tells us that either the nut is bigger than the bolt; the bolt is bigger than the nut; or they are the same size (and so fit together). Because it is dark we are not allowed to compare nuts directly or bolts directly. How many fitting operations do we need to sort the nuts and bolts in the worst case?

Let us try understanding two kinds of algorithms:

- *deterministic* and
- *randomized*

A *deterministic algorithm* is one that always behaves the same way given the same input; the input completely determines the sequence of computations performed by the algorithm.

Normally, when we talk about the running time of an algorithm, we mean the worst-case running time. This is the maximum, over all problems of a certain size, of the running time of that algorithm on that input:

$$T_{worst-case}(n) = max_{|X|=n}T(X)$$

On extremely rare occasions, we will also be interested in the best-case running time:

$$T_{best-case}(n) = min_{|X|=n}T(X)$$

So let us try understanding the meaning of *average case*. The average-case running time is best defined by the expected value, over all inputs X of a certain size, of the algorithm's running time for X:

$$T_{average-case}(n) = \mathbb{E}_{|X|=n}[T(X)] = \sum_{|X|=n}T(X).Pr[X].$$

Randomized algorithms, on the other hand, base their behavior not only on the input but also on several random choices.

The same randomized algorithm, given the same input multiple times, may perform different computations in each invocation. This means, among other things, that the running time of a randomized algorithm on a given input is no longer fixed, but is itself a random variable.

When we analyze randomized algorithms, we are typically interested in the worst-case expected running time. That is, we look at the average running time for each input, and then choose the maximum over all inputs of a certain size:

$$T_{worst-caseexpected}(n) = max_{|X|=n}\mathbb{E}[T(X)].$$

It's important to note here that we are making no assumptions about the probability distribution of possible inputs. All the randomness is inside the algorithm, where we can control it.

Suppose we want to find the nut that matches a particular bolt. The obvious algorithm can be: test every nut until we find a match. This requires exactly *n - 1* tests in the worst case. We might have to check every bolt except one; if we get down the the last bolt without finding a match, we know that the last nut is the one we are looking for.

As far as time complexity of this algorithm is concerned, this algorithm will look at approximately n/2 nuts *on average*.

1.2 Partitioning

It is very much clear by now that the key part in this algorithm is *partition* step as it is in *quicksort*. So before we jump to *randomized* part, let us go through *deterministic* version.

Algorithm 1 Partitioning a sequence

1: **function** PARTITION(a, l, r)
2:     $p \leftarrow a[r]$
3:     $i \leftarrow l - 1$
4:     **for** $j \leftarrow l, r - 1$ **do**
5:       **if** $a[j] \leq p$ **then**
6:         $i \leftarrow i + 1$
7:         $swap(a[i], a[j])$
8:       **end if**
9:     **end for**
10:    **return** $i + 1$
11: **end function**

---

   partition always selects the last element a[r] in the sequence a[l..r] as the *pivot* : partitioning element. It partitions the sequence into four regions, some of which may be empty.

Loop Invariant:

☞ $\forall x \in a[l..i] : x \leq pivot$

☞ $\forall x \in a[i+1..j-1] : x \geq pivot$

☞ a[r] = pivot.

The fourth region is $a[j..r-1]$ which is yet to be evaluated.
Time complexity of *partition* is $\Theta(n)$ where $n = r - l + 1$

Program 1.1: Partitioning in C++

```
1 #include <algorithm>
2 #include <cassert>
3
4 void swap(int *a, int *b)
5 {
6     int t;
7     t = *a;
8     *a = *b;
9     *b = t;
10 }
11
12 int partition(int a[], int l, int r)
13 {
14     int p = a[r];
15     int i = l - 1;
16
```

```
17      for(int  j = 1;  j <= r - 1;  j++)
18      {
19          if(a[j] <= p)
20          {
21              i = i + 1;
22              swap(&a[i], &a[j]);
23          }
24      }
25
26      swap(&a[i + 1], &a[r]);
27
28      return i + 1;
29 }
30
31 int  main()
32 {
33      int a[] =      {8, 1, 6, 4, 0, 3, 9, 5};
34      int aref[] = {1, 4, 0, 3, 5, 8, 9, 6};
35
36      int p = partition(a, 0, 7);
37
38      assert(std::equal(std::begin(a),
39                         std::end(a),
40                         std::begin(aref)));
41      assert(p == 4);
42      assert(a[p] == 5);
43 }
```

1.2.1   STL style partitioning

Program 1.2: STL style implementation of partition

```
1 #include <iostream>
2 #include <algorithm>
3
4 template <typename RandomIter>
5 RandomIter partition(RandomIter l,
6                      RandomIter r)
7 {
8      for(RandomIter j = l;  j < r;  j++)
9      {
10         if(*j <= *r)
11         {
12             std::iter_swap(l++, j);
13         }
14     }
15     std::iter_swap(l, r);
16
17     return l;
18 }
19
20 int  main()
21 {
22     int a[] = {8, 1, 6, 4, 0, 3, 9, 5};
23
24     int *p = partition(a, a + 7);
25
26     std::cout << "Array after partition"
27               << std::endl;
28
29     for(auto e : a)
30     std::cout << e << " ";
31
32     std::cout << std::endl;
33
```

```
34     std :: cout << "partition index : "
35        << std :: distance (std :: begin (a), p) << ", "
36        << "partitioning element : " << *p
37        << std :: endl;
38 }
```

This prints :

```
Array after partition
1 4 0 3 5 8 9 6
partition index : 4, partitioning element : 5
```

1.2.2 std::partition

STL also provides a version of partition algorithm which looks like:

Program 1.3: std::partition

```
1 template <typename BidirectionalIterator ,
2            typename Predicate>
3 BidirectionalIterator
4 partition ( BidirectionalIterator  first ,
5             BidirectionalIterator  last ,
6             Predicate  pred)
7 {
8     while (true)
9     {
10        while (true)
11        {
12            if (first == last)
13                return first ;
14            if (!pred(* first ))
15                break;
16            ++first ;
17        }
18        do
19        {
20            if (first == —last )
21                return first ;
22        } while (!pred(* __last ));
23        std :: iter_swap (first , last );
24        ++first ;
25     }
26 }
```

It places all the elements in the range [first,last) that satisfy predicate before all the elements that do not satisfy it and returns an iterator i such that for any iterator j in the range [first,i) pred(*j) != false, and for any iterator k in the range [i,last), pred(*k) == false. Time complexity is at most (last - first) / 2 swaps.

1.3 Quicksort

Quicksort is a two step divide and conquer based algorithm for sorting a sequence.

1. **Divide** : Partition the sequence $a[l..r]$ into two subsequences $a[l..p-1]$ and $a[p+1, r]$ such that each element of $a[l..p-1] \leq a[p]$ and each element of $a[p+1, r] \geq a[p]$, i.e.
   $\forall x \in a[l..p-1]$ and $\forall y \in a[p+1, r] : x \leq a[p] \leq y$.

2. recursively call quicksort to sort the resulting two sub-sequences in place, namely, $a[l..p-1]$ and $a[p+1, r]$.

Algorithm 2 Quicksort to sort a sequence

```
1: function QUICKSORT(a, l, r)
2:     p ← PARTITION(a, l, r)
3:     QUICKSORT(a, l, p − 1)
4:     QUICKSORT(a, p + 1, r)
5: end function
```

As can be seen easily that running time of quicksort depends on the partitioning of sequence.

Worst case partition(for example in case of sorted sequence as input) will result into two subsequences of lengths n - 1 and 0 respectively.

$$T(n) = T(n − 1) + T(0) + \Theta(n) = T(n − 1) + \Theta(n) = \Theta(n^2)$$

Best case partition will result into almost equal size subsequences every time.

$$T(n) = 2T(n/2) + \Theta(n) = \Theta(n \log n)$$

QUICKSORT's average case is closer to the best case than to the worst case.

To understand it better, let us assume that partitioning always results into subsequences of 9:1 ratio:

$$T(n) = T(9n/10) + T(n/10) + \Theta(n) = \Theta(n \log n)$$

Program 1.4: quicksort in C++

```cpp
#include <iostream>

void swap(int *a, int *b)
{
    int t;
    t = *a;
    *a = *b;
    *b = t;
}

int partition(int a[], int l, int r)
{
    int p = a[r];
    int i = l − 1;

    for(int j = l; j <= r − 1; j++)
    {
        if(a[j] <= p)
        {
            i = i + 1;
            swap(&a[i], &a[j]);
        }
    }

    swap(&a[i + 1], &a[r]);

    return i + 1;
}



void quicksort(int a[], int l, int r)
{
    int p;
    if(l < r)
    {
        p = partition(a, l, r);
        quicksort(a, l, p − 1);
        quicksort(a, p + 1, r);
    }
}
```

```
42
43 int main ()
44 {
45     int a[] = {8, 1, 6, 4, 0, 3, 9, 5};
46
47     quicksort(a, 0, 7);
48
49     std::cout << "Array after sorting"
50               << std::endl;
51
52     for(auto e : a)
53     std::cout << e << " ";
54
55     std::cout << std::endl;
56 }
```

This prints :

```
Array after sorting
0 1 3 4 5 6 8 9
```

1.3.1   STL style Quicksort

Program 1.5: STL style implementation of quicksort

```
1 #include <iostream>
2 #include <algorithm>
3
4 template <typename RandomIter>
5 void quicksort(RandomIter first,
6                RandomIter last)
7 {
8     RandomIter left = first, right = last,
9               pivot = left++;
10
11     if( first != last )
12     {
13         while(left != right)
14         {
15             if(*left < *pivot)
16             {
17                 ++left;
18             }
19             else
20             {
21                 while((left != right)
22                     && (*pivot < *right))
23                     --right;
24
25                 std::iter_swap(left, right);
26             }
27         }
28
29         --left;
30         std::iter_swap(pivot, left);
31
32         quicksort(first, left);
33         quicksort(right, last);
34     }
35 }
36
37 int main ()
38 {
39     int a[] = {8, 1, 6, 4, 0, 3, 9, 5};
```

```
40
41    quicksort(a, a + 7);
42
43    std::cout << "Array after sorting"
44              << std::endl;
45
46    for(auto e : a)
47    std::cout << e << " ";
48
49    std::cout << std::endl;
50 }
```

1.3.2   Quicksort using std::partition

Program 1.6: Implementing quicksort

```
1 #include <algorithm>
2 #include <iterator>
3 #include <functional>
4
5 template <typename RandomaccessIterator>
6 void quicksort(RandomaccessIterator begin,
7                RandomaccessIterator end)
8 {
9     if (begin != end)
10    {
11        RandomaccessIterator pivot =
12            std::partition(begin, end, bind2nd(
13                std::less<typename iterator_traits<
14                    T>::value_type>(), *begin));
15
16        quicksort(begin, pivot);
17        RandomaccessIterator new_pivot = begin;
18        quicksort(++new_pivot, end);
19    }
20 }
```

1.4   Randomized Quicksort

So far we have assumed that all input permutations are equally likely which is true always, hence we add randomization to quicksort. We could randomly shuffle input sequence, but randomized quicksort employs *random sampling*, i.e. chosing element at random, to achieve this. So instead of picking the last element $a[r]$ as pivot, it is picked up randomly from the sequence.

Algorithm 3 Randomized Partition Algorithm
_____
1: **function** RANDOMIZED-PARTITION(a, l, r)
2:     $i \leftarrow random(l, r)$
3:     $swap(a[r], a[i])$
4:     **return** PARTITION(a, l, r)
5: **end function**
_____

Program 1.7: randomized partition in C++

```
1 #include <iostream>
2
3 void swap(int *a, int *b)
4 {
5     int t;
6     t = *a;
7     *a = *b;
```

```
 8        *b = t;
 9  }
10
11  int partition(int a[], int l, int r)
12  {
13        int p = a[r];
14        int i = l - 1;
15
16        for(int j = l; j <= r - 1; j++)
17        {
18            if(a[j] <= p)
19            {
20                i = i + 1;
21                swap(&a[i], &a[j]);
22            }
23        }
24
25        swap(&a[i + 1], &a[r]);
26
27        return i + 1;
28  }
29
30
31  int randomized_partition(int a[], int l, int r)
32  {
33        int i = l + std::rand() % (r - l + 1);
34        swap(&a[r], &a[i]);
35        return partition(a, l, r);
36  }
37
38
39  int main()
40  {
41        int a[] = {8, 1, 6, 4, 0, 3, 9, 5};
42
43        int p = randomized_partition(a, 0, 7);
44
45        std::cout <<
46        "Array after randomized partition"
47        << std::endl;
48
49        for(auto e : a)
50        std::cout << e << " ";
51
52        std::cout << std::endl;
53
54        std::cout
55            << "partition index : " << p << ", "
56            << "partitioning element : "
57            << a[p] << std::endl;
58  }
```

Output of this program is:

```
Array after randomized partition
1 4 0 3 5 8 9 6
partition index : 4, partitioning element : 5
```

Randomly selecting the pivot element will result into reasonably well balanced partitioned subsequences on average.

Algorithm 4 Randomized Quicksort Algorithm

1: **function** RANDOMIZED-QUICKSORT(a, l, r)
2:     $p \leftarrow$ RANDOMIZED-PARTITION(a, l, r)
3:     RANDOMIZED-QUICKSORT$(a, l, p - 1)$
4:     RANDOMIZED-QUICKSORT$(a, p + 1, r)$
5: **end function**

Randomization of quicksort stops any specific type of sequence from causing worst- case behavior. For example, an already-sorted array causes worst-case behavior in non randomized quicksort, but not in randomized-quicksort.

In each level of recursion, the partition obtained by RANDOMIZED-PARTITION puts any constant fraction of the elements on one side of the partition, then the recursion tree has depth $\theta(\log n)$, and $O(n)$ work is performed at each level. Even if we add new levels with the most unbalanced partition possible between these levels, the total time remains $O(n \log n)$.

We can analyze the expected running time of RANDOMIZED-QUICKSORT precisely by first understanding how the partitioning procedure operates and then using this understanding to derive an $O(n \log n)$ bound on the expected running time. This upper bound on the expected running time, combined with the $\theta(n \log n)$ best-case bound we saw earlier, yields a $O(n \log n)$ expected running time.

Thus time complexity of randomized-quicksort $O(n \log n)$.

Program 1.8: randomized quicksort in C++

```cpp
#include <iostream>

void swap(int *a, int *b)
{
    int t;
    t = *a;
    *a = *b;
    *b = t;
}

int partition(int a[], int l, int r)
{
    int p = a[r];
    int i = l - 1;

    for(int j = l; j <= r - 1; j++)
    {
        if(a[j] <= p)
        {
            i = i + 1;
            swap(&a[i], &a[j]);
        }
    }

    swap(&a[i + 1], &a[r]);

    return i + 1;
}



int randomized_partition(int a[], int l,
                                  int r)
{
    int i = l + std::rand() % (r - l + 1);
    swap(&a[r], &a[i]);
    return partition(a, l, r);
}
```

```
38
39
40 void randomized_quicksort(int a[], int l,
41                                      int r)
42 {
43     int p;
44     if(l < r)
45     {
46         p = randomized_partition(a, l, r);
47         randomized_quicksort(a, l, p - 1);
48         randomized_quicksort(a, p + 1, r);
49     }
50 }
51
52
53 int main()
54 {
55     int a[] = {8, 1, 6, 4, 0, 3, 9, 5};
56
57     randomized_quicksort(a, 0, 7);
58
59     std::cout << "Array after sorting"
60               << std::endl;
61
62     for(auto e : a)
63         std::cout << e << " ";
64
65     std::cout << std::endl;
66 }
```

Output of this program is:

```
Array after sorting
0 1 3 4 5 6 8 9
```

1.5 Deterministic Algorithm for nuts n bolts

Unfortunately, it seems much harder to find an efficient deterministic algorithm for nuts and bolts problem. The first $O(n \log^{O(1)} n)$-time deterministic algorithm was by Alon et al. [2] which is also based on Quicksort and takes $\Theta(n \log^4 n)$ time. To find a good pivot element which splits the problem into two subproblems of nearly the same size, they run $\log n$ iterations of a procedure which eliminates half of the nuts in each iteration while maintaining at least one good pivot; since there is only one nut left in the end, this one must be a good pivot. This procedure uses the edges of an efficient expander of degree $\Theta(\log^2 n)$ to define its comparisons. Therefore, finding a good pivot takes $\Theta(n \log^3 n)$ time, and the entire Quicksort takes $\Theta(n \log^4 n)$ time. Alon et al. [2] mention two potential applications of the nuts and bolts problem:

1. local sorting of nodes in a given graph

2. selection of read only memory with a little read/write memory

Phillip G. Bradford has a given a simple deterministic algorithm [3] for solving the nuts and bolts problem that makes $O(n \log n)$ nut-and-bolt comparisons. This algorithm is based on certain expander based comparator networks and it demonstrates the existence of a decision tree with depth $O(n \log n)$ that solves this problem. They do this by showing that comparator networks that are $\epsilon - halvers$ exist for nuts and bolts. An $\epsilon - halvers$ approximately splits a set of n elements with $O(n)$ complexity. This approximate splitting is enough to allow this algorithm to select good pivots while iterating $\epsilon - halvers$ on geometrically smaller sets of nuts and bolts. The hard part in building these $\epsilon - halvers$ is to ensure that nuts are never compared to nuts and bolts are never compared to bolts while maintaining the $\epsilon - halving$ property. Let $S = s_1, \ldots, s_n$ be a set of nuts of different sizes and $B = b_1, \ldots, b_n$ be a set of corresponding bolts.

For a nut $s \in S$ define rank(s) as $|t \in B| s \geq t|$. The rank of a bolt is defined similarly.

For a constant $c < \frac{1}{2}$, s is called a *c-approximate median* if $cn \leq rank)s) \leq (1-c)n$. Similarly, define the *relative rank* of s with respect to a subset $T \in B$ as $rank_T(s) := \frac{|t \in T| s \geq t|}{|T|}$.

The algorithm for matching nuts and bolts works as follows:

- ☞ Find a c-approximate median s of the n given nuts (constant c will be determined later). This requires $O(n)$ nut-and-bolt comparisons.
- ☞ Find the bolt b corresponding to s.
- ☞ Compare all nuts to b and all bolts to s. This gives two piles of nuts (and bolts as well), one with the nuts (bolts) smaller than s and one with the nuts (bolts) bigger than s.
- ☞ Run the algorithm recursively on the two piles of the smaller nuts and bolts and the two piles of the bigger nuts and bolts.

Please note that this algorithm can match n nuts with their corresponding bolts in $O(n \log n)$ nut-and-bolt comparisons because each subproblem has size at most $(1 - c)n$, hence the depth of the recursion is only $O(n \log n)$, and in each level of the recursion the total number of nut-and-bolt comparisons to get all of the c-approximate medians in $O(n)$.

Let us summarize the components of this algorithm as follows.

Algorithm 5 Selecting a c-approximate median of X with O(n) complexity

---

1: **function** GET-C-APPROXIMATE-MEDIAN(X)
2:     $n \leftarrow \frac{|X_0|}{2}$
3:     $l \leftarrow 1$
4:     $r \leftarrow 2n$
5:     $i \leftarrow 0$
6:     **while** $|X_i| \geq C$ **do**
7:        $Y_i \leftarrow$ nut-and-bolt-ϵ-halve(X_i)
8:        $B \leftarrow$ BACK-TRACK(Y_i, i, Z)
9:        $Z \leftarrow$ FIND-MISPLACED-ELEMENTS $\left(Y_i, i, \frac{n}{2^i}\right)$
10:        **if** i is odd **then**
11:           $r \leftarrow \frac{(l+r)}{2}$
12:        **else**
13:           $l \leftarrow \frac{(l+r)}{2}$
14:        **end if**
15:        $i \leftarrow i + 1$
16:        $X_i \leftarrow Y_{i-1}[l, r] \cup Z \cup B$
17:     **end while**
18:     **return** X_i
19: **end function**

Algorithm 6 Back-Tracking

1: **function** BACK-TRACKING(Y, i, Z)
2:    **if** $i \leq 2$ **then**
3:       **return** $\emptyset$
4:    **end if**
5:    **if** i is even **then**
6:

      for any members of Z that are in the right half of Y find all members of all of the left fringes that are supported exclusively by these members of Z or other active elements. Put these candidate illicitly supported elements in B.

7:    **else**
8:

      for any members of Z that are in the left half of Y find all members of all of the right fringes that are supported exclusively by these members of Z or other active elements. Put these candidate illicitly supported elements in B.

9:    **end if**
10:    **return** B
11: **end function**

Algorithm 7 Finding Misplaced Nuts and Bolts

1: **function** FIND-MISPLACED-ELEMENTS(X, i, m)
2:    $r \leftarrow |X|$
3:    $l \leftarrow 1$
4:    **if** i is odd **then**
5:       $Z_1 \leftarrow X\left[\frac{(l+r)}{2}, r\right]$
6:    **else**
7:       $Z_1 \leftarrow X\left[l, \frac{(l+r)}{2}\right]$
8:    **end if**
9:    $j \leftarrow 1$
10:    **while** $|Z_j| \geq K\epsilon m$ **do**
11:       $Z_j \leftarrow$ nut-and-bolt-ϵ-halve($Z_j[l, r]$)
12:       **if** i is odd **then**
13:          $r \leftarrow r - \frac{(l+r)}{2}$
14:       **else**$l \leftarrow l + \frac{(l+r)}{2}$
15:       **end if**
16:       $Z_j \leftarrow (Z_j[l, r])$
17:       $j \leftarrow j + 1$
18:    **end while**
19:    **return** Z_j
20: **end function**

1.6 Remarks

In this chapter, we discussed the design and implementation of a randomized version of QUICKSORT algorithm for solving the nuts and bolts problem in $O(n \log n)$ nut-and-bolt matching operations. There are huge constants hidden in the asymptotic notation here, though those are not discussed explicitly in this chapter. Reducing these constants (perhaps by removing the expanders) would be an interesting endeavor in itself. This is left an exercise to the interested reader.

Chapter 2

Searching two-dimensional sorted array

Problem 2 (*David Gries*)

*Design and implement an efficient algorithm to search for a given integer x in a 2-dimensional **sorted** array a[0..m][0..n]. Please note that it is sorted row-wise and column-wise in ascending order.*

Solution

2.1 Basic Analysis

Let us start analyzing the problem by looking at implied properties related to search space. This array has the following properties:

1. no of rows $m \geq 1$
2. no of columns $n \geq 1$
3. Entries in each row are ordered by $\leq$, i.e., for $0 \leq i < m$ && $0 \leq j < n$

$$\boxed{a[i][j] \leq a[i][j+1]}$$

- $a_{11} \leq a_{12} \leq \ldots \leq a_{1n}$
- $a_{21} \leq a_{22} \leq \ldots \leq a_{2n}$

  $\vdots$

- $a_{m1} \leq a_{m2} \leq \ldots \leq a_{mn}$

4. Entries in each column are ordered by $\leq$, i.e., for $0 \leq i < m$ && for $0 \leq j < n$

$$\boxed{a[i][j] \leq a[i+1][j]}$$

- $a_{11} \leq a_{21} \leq \ldots \leq a_{m1}$
- $a_{12} \leq a_{22} \leq \ldots \leq a_{m2}$

  $\vdots$

- $a_{1n} \leq a_{2n} \leq \ldots \leq a_{mn}$

Pictorial representation of two-dimensional sorted array is as follows:

With the properties above, we have to develop an efficient algorithm to find the position of a given integer x in the array a, i.e., the algorithm should find i and j such that $\boxed{\mathbf{x = a[i,j]}}$. By efficient we mean to minimize the number of comparisons as much as possible.

Let us treat the input array as some kind of a rectangular region.

The problem demands that the integer x does exist somewhere in this region. Let us label this condition as *Input Assertion* or *Precondition*.

2.2 Precondition (aka *Input Assertion*)

$\boxed{\mathbf{x \in a[0..m-1, 0..n-1]}}$

i.e., x is present somewhere in this rectangular region a.

After the program terminates successfully, x has to be found in a rectangular region of a where the rectangular region consists of just one row and column. Let us label this condition as *Output Assertion* or *Result Assertion* or *Postcondition*.

2.3 Postcondition (aka *Result Assertion)*

$\boxed{\mathbf{0 \leq i \leq m-1}}$ && $\boxed{\mathbf{0 \leq j \leq n-1}}$ && $\boxed{\mathbf{x = a[i,j]}}$

i.e., x is in a rectangular region of a where the rectangular region consists of just one row and column, i.e., x is present at i^{th} row and j^{th} column of a.

2.4 Invariant

Looking at the precondition and postcondition, it is not that difficult to figure out that during the execution of our algorithm, x is guaranteed to be confined within some rectangular region of a, i.e.,

$0 \le i \le p \le m-1$ &&

$0 \le q \le j \le n-1$ &&

$x \in a[i..p, q..j]$.

In simple words, the invariant implies that

- We have exhausted the rows a[0..p-1] and x is not present in these already searched rows.
- We have exhausted the columns a[0..q-1] and x is not present in these already searched columns.

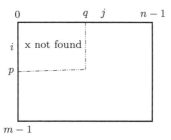

2.5 Contract the rectangular region

We have to choose a rectangular region $a[i..p, q..j]$ that contains x followed by making this region smaller till x is found.

Initial bounded searcheable region is represented by :
$i = 0 \quad p = m-1 \quad q = 0 \quad j = n-1$

Looking at bounds of the rectangle, there are 4 ways to march towards contracting it:

- if $a[i, j] < x$ then since the row is ordered $\implies i \leftarrow i + 1$, because if $a[i, j] > x$, then all the entries of that row is also greater than x. Please note that its execution will maintain the stated invariant if x is not found in a[i, 0..n-1], i.e., in i^{th} row.
- if $a[p, q] > x \implies p \leftarrow p - 1$
- if $a[p, q] < x \implies q \leftarrow q + 1$

• if $a[i,j] > x \implies j \leftarrow j - 1$

These conditions are also known as *guards*[4].

2.6   Saddleback Search Algorithm

Let us put together the complete solution as shown below:

Algorithm 8 Saddleback Search Algorithm

1: **PreCondition** : $x \in a[0..m-1, 0..n-1]$
2: **PostCondition** : $0 \leq i \leq m-1 \ \&\& \ 0 \leq j \leq n-1 \ \&\& \ x = a[i,j]$
3: **function** SADDLEBACK-SEARCH(a[0..m-1, 0..n-1], x)
4:      $i \leftarrow 0$
5:      $p \leftarrow m - 1$
6:      $q \leftarrow 0$
7:      $j \leftarrow n - 1$
8:      **Invariant** : $0 \leq i \leq p \leq m - 1 \ \&\& \ 0 \leq q \leq j \leq n - 1 \ \&\&$ $x \in a[i..p, q..j]$
9:      **while** $x \neq a[i,j]$ **do**
10:         **if** a[i, j] < x **then**
11:             $i \longleftarrow i + 1$
12:         **end if**
13:         **if** a[p, q] > x **then**
14:             $p \longleftarrow p - 1$
15:         **end if**
16:         **if** a[p, q] < x **then**
17:             $q \longleftarrow q + 1$
18:         **end if**
19:         **if** a[i, j] > x **then**
20:             $j \longleftarrow j - 1$
21:         **end if**
22:      **end while**
23: **end function**

This layout was simple enough to embark on the journey of solving problems using formal programming methodology in somewhat pragmatic manner.

With the above setting in place, now it is time to think towards proving correctness of the result upon termination. As an astute reader, it is not that difficult to surmise that intermediate conditions in form of the points p,q of search space are not really needed to test veracity of the result upon termination. Only the first and last conditions are necessary and sufficient enough to prove it. So let us drop the middle (two) conditions to complete the working program in practice as following:

Algorithm 9 Saddleback Search Algorithm in practice

1: **PreCondition** : $x \in a[0..m-1, 0..n-1]$
2: **PostCondition** : $0 \le i \le m-1$ && $0 \le j \le n-1$ && $x = a[i,j]$
3: **Invariant** : x is in a[i..m-1, 0..j]
4: **function** SADDLEBACK-SEARCH(a[0..m-1, 0..n-1], x)
5:     **while** $x \ne a[i,j]$ **do**
6:         **if** a[i, j] < x **then**
7:             $i \leftarrow i + 1$
8:         **else** $j \leftarrow j - 1$
9:         **end if**
10:     **end while**
11: **end function**

Still, we need to address that why we chose to start from top rightmost corner. We can of course start from bottom leftmost corner as well. We leave this an exercise to the reader to work out and think about the pros n cons of choosing the starting point.

2.6.1   C++11 Implementation

Let us try programming this algorithm in a real language, say C++11 to bring ourselves at workplace-setting environment:

Program 2.1: Saddleback search in C++11

```cpp
#include <algorithm>
#include <array>

using Point = std::pair<int, int>;

template <int m, int n>
using TwoDimArray
    = std::array<std::array<int, n>, m>;

template <int m, int n>
Point saddleback_search(TwoDimArray<m, n> & a,
                        int x)
{
    Point p(-1, -1);

    int i = 0, j = n - 1;

    while(x != a[i][j])
    {
        if(a[i][j] < x) i += 1;
        else j -= 1;
    }

    p.first = i;
    p.second = j;

    return p;
}
```

Program 2.2: Using Saddleback Search

```cpp
#include "saddleback_search.hpp"
#include <iostream>

int main()
{
    TwoDimArray<4, 4> a = {
                           2, 2, 3, 5,
```

```
 8                                      3, 4, 5, 6,
 9                                      3, 5, 6, 8,
10                                      3, 6, 7, 9
11                                 };
12
13      Point p = saddleback_search <4, 4>(a, 6);
14
15      std::cout << "6 is found at : a["
16                << p.first << "]["
17                << p.second << "]"
18                << std::endl;
19
20 }
```

Output of the program is:

```
6 is found at : a[1][3]
```

2.6.2   Time Complexity

As could be seen that the number of comparisons required in Saddleback search algorithm is at most $n + m$. Hence time complexity is $O(n + m)$.

How to improve it further, is it possible?

Let us take a simple case as a tryst to understand it better. Let us assume that the array is a square one with n x n dimension, i.e., m = n. Please note that the elements lying off-diagonal in the rectangular region form an unordered sequence of integers, i.e., a[0, n-1], a[1, n-2], a[2, n-3], ..., a[n-2, 1] and a[n-1, 0] form an unordered list because this particular sequence is not affected at all by the imposed ordering on row and column respectively. So even if we assume that x could be lying on this off-diagonal set, then at least n comparisons are required in the worst case.

Have we done our bit fully ? Not yet. We request our reader to think about it and be patient for now, thoughts on possible improvement will be taken up soon, whether it is feasible to improve it further or not will reveal itself in due course of time. But for now, we think about a simple variation in the problem statement and try solving it with help of approach discussed so far.

2.7   Variation

As mentioned in the problem statement, it was desired to find any one in case of multiple occurrence of the value sought after. How about finding all of these instead ? This problem is one of the variations of *saddleback search*(discussed in the previous section). Here instead of locating an occurrence, it counts the number of occurrences.

2.7.1   Find First Occurrence

Before we march ahead towards a solution, we need to work on a strategy to spot the very first occurrence of x, because the earlier approach was focused to find any occurrence in case of multiple ones. So if we try to build our logic on the earlier approach, we may miss few occurrences.

Therefore, we have to be a little more judicious in starting point which cannot simply be set to either rightmost top corner or leftmost bottom corner.

To understand it better, let us stick to our earlier solution for now as illustrated ahead and take it from there towards an appropriate solution.

We have to design an efficient algorithm to search for a given integer x in a 2-dimensional **sorted** array a[0..m][0..n]. Please note that it is sorted row-wise and column-wise in ascending order. In case of multiple occurrences, please find the very first occurrence, i.e, the occurrence with the smallest value of the row index and at the same time the occurrence with the smallest value of the column index as well. Please note that row index and column index at topmost left corner is being treated as (0, 0).

1. Find any occurrence using original saddleback search algorithm which finds the entry corresponding to smallest row index and highest column index, i.e., it finds the very first row containing that value but the column index depict the last most occurrence in that particular row.

2. Search backwards to adjust the column index to point to lowest index corresponding to that entry in that row.

Algorithm 10 Saddleback Search Algorithm : Find First Occurrence

---
1: **function** SADDLEBACK-SEARCH(a[0..m-1, 0..n-1], x)
2:     $i \leftarrow 0$
3:     $j \leftarrow n - 1$
4:     **while** $x \neq a[i,j]$ **do**
5:         **if** a[i, j] < x **then**
6:             $i \leftarrow i + 1$
7:         **else if** a[i, j] > x **then**f
8:             $j \leftarrow j - 1$
9:         **end if**
10:     **end while**
11:     **while** $x == a[i,j]$ **do**
12:         $j \leftarrow j - 1$
13:     **end while**
14:     $j \leftarrow j + 1$
15: **end function**

Program 2.3: Saddleback Search : First Occurrence

```
1 #include <algorithm>
2 #include <array>
3
4 using Point = std::pair<int, int>;
5
6 template <int m, int n>
7 using TwoDimArray
8     = std::array<std::array<int, n>, m>;
9
10 template <int m, int n>
11 Point saddleback_search_first (TwoDimArray<m, n>
12                               & a, int x)
13 {
14     Point p(-1, -1);
15
16     int i = 0, j = n - 1;
17
18     while(x != a[i][j])
19     {
20         if(a[i][j] < x) ++i;
21         else --j;
22     }
23
24     while(x == a[i][j]) --j;
25
26     ++j;
```

```
27
28      p.first = i;
29      p.second = j;
30
31      return p;
32 }
```

Program 2.4: Using Saddleback Search : First Occurrence

```
1 #include "saddleback_search_first.hpp"
2 #include <iostream>
3
4 int main()
5 {
6      TwoDimArray<4, 4> a = {
7                             2, 2, 3, 5,
8                             3, 4, 6, 6,
9                             3, 5, 6, 6,
10                            3, 6, 6, 9
11                           };
12
13     Point p
14        = saddleback_search_first<4, 4>(a, 6);
15
16     std::cout << "6 is found at : a["
17               << p.first << "]["
18               << p.second << "]"
19               << std::endl;
20
21 }
```

It prints:

```
6 is found at : a[1][2]
```

First part of this algorithm uses original saddleback search whose complexity is $O(n + m)$. Second part involves linear search in backward dimension in the given row $\implies O(n)$. Hence time complexity of *Saddleback Search : Find First Occurrence* is $O(n + m)$. Please note that second part of this algorithm can be accomplished using binary search. We leave this an exercise to the reader.

2.7.2 Find All Occurrences

Before we undertake solving the problem of finding the count of x, let us turn our attention to a related twister which requires reporting of all the occurrences of a given integer x in the array a[m, n], i.e., it will report all the row-indices (i) and column-indices (j) of the array where $x == a[i, j]$.

So far our termination condition was derived upon the first occurrence of x in the array, but now we need to modify to proceed further till array is completely exhausted and maintain a list of vertices found relevant so far.

Algorithm 11 Saddleback Search Algorithm : Find All Occurrences

1: **function** SADDLEBACK-FINDALL(a[0..m-1, 0..n-1], x)
2: $\quad i \leftarrow 0$
3: $\quad j \leftarrow n - 1$
4: $\quad currrent\_col\_index \leftarrow j$
5: $\quad List < Pair < rowindex, columnindex >> list\_indices$
6: $\quad$ **while** $j \leq n - 1$ **do**
7: $\quad\quad$ **if** a[i, j] < x **then**
8: $\quad\quad\quad i \leftarrow i + 1$
9: $\quad\quad$ **else if** a[i, j] > x **then**
10: $\quad\quad\quad j \leftarrow j - 1$
11: $\quad\quad$ **else if** a[i, j] == x **then**
12: $\quad\quad\quad currrent\_col\_index \leftarrow j$
13: $\quad\quad\quad$ **while** currrent_col_index ≥ 0 **and** a[i][currrent_col_index] == x **do**
14: $\quad\quad\quad\quad$ list_indices.insert(Pair<rowindex, columnindex>(i, currrent_col_index))
15: $\quad\quad\quad\quad currrent\_col\_index \leftarrow currrent\_col\_index - 1$
16: $\quad\quad\quad$ **end while**
17: $\quad\quad\quad i \leftarrow i + 1$
18: $\quad\quad$ **end if**
19: $\quad$ **end while**
20: **end function**

Key thing to notice here is how to start the next search after first occurrence is reported, say a[i, j] ?

If x is equal to a[i, j] for a given row index i and column index j, then it is obvious that these correspond to smallest values of row and column indices. Our algorithm developed for finding the first occurrence ends up traversing the path from the last most to first most in a given row, so all we need to do is to record this path and march towards the next row.

Program 2.5: Saddleback Find All

```
1 #include <algorithm>
2 #include <array>
3 #include <vector>
4
5 template <int m, int n>
6 using TwoDimArray
7     = std::array<std::array<int, n>, m>;
8
9 typedef std::pair<int, int> PairIndices;
10
11 typedef std::vector<PairIndices> ListIndices;
12
13 template <int m, int n>
14 ListIndices saddleback_findall(
15                 TwoDimArray<m, n> & a, int x)
16 {
17     size_t i = 0, j = n - 1;
18     ListIndices list_indices;
19     int currrent_col_index = j;
20
21     while(j <= n - 1)
22     {
23         if(a[i][j] < x) i += 1;
24         else if(a[i][j] > x) j -= 1;
25         else // a[i][j] == x
26         {
```

```
27          currrent_col_index = j;
28          while(currrent_col_index >=0 &&
29                  a[i][currrent_col_index] == x)
30          list_indices.push_back(
31        PairIndices(i, currrent_col_index--));
32
33            ++i;
34        }
35    }
36
37    return list_indices;
38 }
```

Program 2.6: Using Saddleback Find All

```
1 #include "saddleback_findall.hpp"
2 #include <iostream>
3
4 int main()
5 {
6    TwoDimArray<4, 4> a = {
7                              2, 2, 3, 5,
8                              3, 4, 5, 6,
9                              3, 5, 6, 8,
10                             3, 6, 7, 9
11                         };
12
13   ListIndices indexList
14       = saddleback_findall<4, 4>(a, 6);
15
16   std::cout << "6 is found at : \n";
17   for(PairIndices & p : indexList)
18   std::cout << "a[" << p.first << "]"
19             << "[" << p.second << "]"
20             << std::endl;
21 }
```

It prints :

```
6 is found at :
a[1][3]
a[2][2]
a[3][1]
```

Program 2.7: Another Usage of Saddleback Find All

```
1 #include "saddleback_findall.hpp"
2 #include <iostream>
3
4 int main()
5 {
6    TwoDimArray<4, 4> a = {
7                              2, 2, 3, 5,
8                              3, 4, 6, 6,
9                              3, 5, 6, 6,
10                             3, 6, 6, 9
11                         };
12
13   ListIndices indexList
14       = saddleback_findall<4, 4>(a, 6);
15
16   std::cout << "6 is found at : \n";
17   for(PairIndices & p : indexList)
18   std::cout << "a[" << p.first << "]"
```

```
19                          << "[" << p.second << "]"
20                          << std::endl;
21 }
```

It prints :

```
6 is found at :
a[1][3]
a[1][2]
a[2][3]
a[2][2]
a[3][2]
a[3][1]
```

Program 2.8: Continue Using Saddleback Find All

```
 1 #include "saddleback_findall.hpp"
 2 #include <iostream>
 3
 4 int main()
 5 {
 6     TwoDimArray<4, 4> a = {
 7                             6, 6, 6, 6,
 8                             6, 6, 6, 6,
 9                             6, 6, 6, 6,
10                             6, 6, 6, 6
11                           };
12
13     ListIndices indexList
14         = saddleback_findall<4, 4>(a, 6);
15
16     std::cout << "6 is found at : \n";
17     for(PairIndices & p : indexList)
18     std::cout << "a[" << p.first << "]"
19               << "[" << p.second << "]"
20               << std::endl;
21 }
```

It prints :

```
6 is found at :
a[0][3]
a[0][2]
a[0][1]
a[0][0]
a[1][3]
a[1][2]
a[1][1]
a[1][0]
a[2][3]
a[2][2]
a[2][1]
a[2][0]
a[3][3]
a[3][2]
a[3][1]
a[3][0]
```

Time Complexity is $O(mn)$.

2.7.3 Saddleback Count

Now our task becomes easier to work out original problem posed earlier, i.e., finding the count of a given integer x in the array a.

Algorithm 12 Saddleback Count Algorithm : Initial Approach

1: **function** SADDLEBACK-COUNT($a[0..m-1, 0..n-1]$, x)
2: $\quad i \leftarrow 0$
3: $\quad j \leftarrow n - 1$
4: $\quad count \leftarrow 0$
5: $\quad$ **while** $j \leq n - 1$ **do**
6: $\quad\quad$ **if** a[i, j] < x **then**
7: $\quad\quad\quad i \leftarrow i + 1$
8: $\quad\quad$ **else if** a[i, j] > x **then**
9: $\quad\quad\quad j \leftarrow j - 1$
10: $\quad\quad$ **else if** a[i, j] == x **then**
11: $\quad\quad\quad i \leftarrow i + 1$
12: $\quad\quad\quad j \leftarrow j - 1$
13: $\quad\quad\quad count \leftarrow count + 1$
14: $\quad\quad$ **end if**
15: $\quad$ **end while**
16: **end function**

Program 2.9: Saddleback Count : Initial Approach

```cpp
#include <algorithm>
#include <array>

template <int m, int n>
using TwoDimArray
    = std::array<std::array<int, n>, m>;

template <int m, int n>
size_t saddleback_count(
    TwoDimArray<m, n> & a, int x)
{
    size_t i = 0, j = n - 1, count = 0;

    while(j <= n - 1)
    {
        if(a[i][j] < x) i += 1;
        else if(a[i][j] > x) j -= 1;
        else // a[i][j] == x
        {
            count += 1;
            i += 1;
            j -= 1;
        }
    }

    return count;
}
```

Program 2.10: Using Saddleback Count

```cpp
#include "saddleback_count.hpp"
#include <iostream>

int main()
{
```

```
 6        TwoDimArray<4, 4> a = {
 7                                    2, 2, 3, 5,
 8                                    3, 4, 5, 6,
 9                                    3, 5, 6, 8,
10                                    3, 6, 7, 9
11                            };
12
13        size_t count
14             = saddleback_count<4, 4>(a, 6);
15
16        std::cout << "Count of 6 is: "
17                     << count << std::endl;
18 }
```

It prints : Count of 6 is: 3 which is fine so far.

Let us take another example:

Program 2.11: Using Saddleback Count : Count of 6 should be 6

```
 1 #include "saddleback_count.hpp"
 2 #include <iostream>
 3
 4 int main()
 5 {
 6        TwoDimArray<4, 4> a = {
 7                                    2, 2, 3, 5,
 8                                    3, 4, 6, 6,
 9                                    3, 5, 6, 6,
10                                    3, 6, 6, 9
11                            };
12
13        size_t count
14             = saddleback_count<4, 4>(a, 6);
15
16        std::cout << "Count of 6 is: "
17                     << count << std::endl;
18 }
```

This too prints : Count of 6 is: 3 which is wrong because it should print : Count of 6 is: 6.

As an astute reader, you can figure out that ordering of rows and columns plays a key role here. Saddleback search has to locate such an occurrence, more precisely, the occurrence with the smallest value of the row index and at the same time the occurrence with the smallest value of the column index as well. Please note that the earlier logic relied on locating the occurrence with the smallest value of the row index and at the same time the occurrence with the largest value of the column index. So let us use the insight gained in the solution of finding first occurrence followed by finding all the occurrences of saddleback search with necessary modifications.

Algorithm 13 Saddleback Count : Correct Algorithm

1: **function** SADDLEBACK-COUNT(a[0..m-1, 0..n-1], x)
2:     $i \leftarrow 0$
3:     $j \leftarrow n - 1$
4:     $currrent\_col\_index \leftarrow j$
5:     $count \leftarrow 0$
6:     **while** $j \leq n - 1$ **do**
7:       **if** a[i, j] < x **then**
8:         $i \leftarrow i + 1$
9:       **else if** a[i, j] > x **then**
10:        $j \leftarrow j - 1$
11:       **else if** a[i, j] == x **then**
12:         $currrent\_col\_index \leftarrow j$
13:         **while** currrent_col_index ≥ 0 **and** a[i][currrent_col_index] == x **do**
14:           $count \leftarrow count + 1$
15:           $currrent\_col\_index \leftarrow currrent\_col\_index - 1$
16:         **end while**
17:         $i \leftarrow i + 1$
18:       **end if**
19:     **end while**
20:     **return** count
21: **end function**

Program 2.12: Implementing Saddleback Count

```cpp
#include <algorithm>
#include <array>

template <int m, int n>
using TwoDimArray
    = std::array<std::array<int, n>, m>;

template <int m, int n>
size_t saddleback_count(
    TwoDimArray<m, n> & a, int x)
{
    size_t i = 0, j = n - 1, count = 0;
    int current_col_index = j;

    while(j <= n - 1)
    {
        if(a[i][j] < x) i += 1;
        else if(a[i][j] > x) j -= 1;
        else // a[i][j] == x
        {
            current_col_index = j;
            while(current_col_index >=0 &&
              a[i][current_col_index] == x)
            {
                ++count;
                current_col_index--;
            }
            ++i;
        }
    }

    return count;
}
```

Program 2.13: Using Saddleback Count

```cpp
#include "saddleback_count_correct.hpp"
#include <iostream>

int main()
{
    TwoDimArray<4, 4> a = {
                            2, 2, 3, 5,
                            3, 4, 6, 6,
                            3, 5, 6, 6,
                            3, 6, 6, 9
                          };

    size_t count
        = saddleback_count<4, 4>(a, 6);

    std::cout << "Count of 6 is: "
              << count << std::endl;
}
```

It prints :

```
Count of 6 is: 6
```

Program 2.14: another Usage of Saddleback Count

```cpp
#include "saddleback_count_correct.hpp"
#include <iostream>

int main()
{
    TwoDimArray<4, 4> a = {
                            6, 6, 6, 6,
                            6, 6, 6, 6,
                            6, 6, 6, 6,
                            6, 6, 6, 6
                          };

    size_t count
        = saddleback_count<4, 4>(a, 6);

    std::cout << "Count of 6 is: "
              << count << std::endl;
}
```

It prints :

```
Count of 6 is: 16
```

Time complexity is same as that of find all, i.e., $O(mn)$.

2.8   Remarks

It is called *Saddleback Search* because the search space is confined by a region with the smallest element at the top-left, largest at bottom-right and two wings gives it a look like a saddle.

Chapter 3

Lowest Common Ancestor(LCA) Problem

Problem 3 (*Tarjan*)

Find the lowest common ancestor(aka lca), i.e., ancestor with maximal depth, of a pair of nodes in a rooted tree.

Solution

3.1 Basic Analysis

In a rooted tree T, a node u is an *ancestor* of a node v if u is on the unique path from the root to v. It can be easily inferred from this definition that a node is an ancestor of itself. A *proper ancestor* of v refers to an ancestor that is not v.

In a rooted tree T, the *lowest common ancestor(aka lca)* of two nodes x and y is the deepest node in T that is an ancestor of both x and y.

LCA problem is one of the most fundamental algorithmic problems on trees and it has been intensively studied mainly due to:

- It is inherently algorithmically beautiful.
- Fast algorithms for the LCA problem can be used to solve other algorithmic problems.

The set of ancestors $a(u)$ of a node $u \in V$ is defined as:

$$a(u) = \begin{cases} \{x\} \cup a(parent(x)), & x \neq root \\ \{x\} & \text{otherwise} \end{cases}$$

where parent(x) is the parent of a node x in the tree.

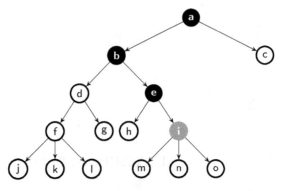

In the tree drawn above, $a(i) = \{i, e, b, a\}$

The set of common ancestors $ca(u, v)$ of nodes u and v is defined as

$$ca(u, v) = a(u) \cap a(v)$$

The lowest common ancestors $lca(u, v)$ is a common ancestor of u and v with maximal depth, i.e. order common ancestors $ca(u, v) = \{x_1, \ldots, x_k\}$ according to their level:

$$l(x_1) < l(x_2) < l(x_3) \ldots < l(x_k)$$

where $l(u)$ is the level of a node, x_1 is the root vertex r and x_k is the *least common ancestor*.

Properties of the lowest common ancestor can be summarized as:

- $lca(\{u\}) = u$
- *Identity* : $\forall u \in V : lca(u, u) = u$
- *Commutativity* : $\forall \{u, v\} \subseteq V \times V : lca(u, v) = lca(v, u)$
- Number of different lca pairs

$$\binom{n}{2} = \frac{n(n-1)}{2}$$

- If neither u nor v is an ancestor of the other, than u and v lie in different immediate subtrees of $lca(u, v)$, i.e., the child of the *lca* of which u is a descendant is not the same as the child of the *lca* of which v is a descendant.). Please note that the *lca* is the only node in the tree for which this is true.
- The entire set of common ancestors of $S = \{v_1, v_2, \ldots, v_n\}$ is given by $lca(S)$ and all of its ancestors (all the way up to the root of the tree). In particular, every common ancestor of S is an ancestor of $lca(S)$.
- $lca(S)$ precedes all nodes in S in the tree's preordering, and follows all nodes in S in the tree's postordering.
- If $S = A \cup B$ with A and B both nonempty, then $lca(S) = lca(lca(A), lca(B))$. For example, $lca(u,v,w) = lca(u,lca(v,w))$. (The *lca* shares this property with the similar-sounding *lowest common multiple* and *greatest common divisor*; and this property can be used to compute the emphlca of arbitrarily large sets using only binary *lca* computations.)
- $d(u, v) = h(u) + h(v) - 2h(lca(u, v))$, where d represents the distance between two nodes and h represents the height of a node.

3.2   Simple Solution

Given P as parent of a node and r as the root of the tree, we can easily find lca of the nodes u and v by computing these two sequences:

1. $u, P(u), P(P(u)), \ldots, r$
2. $v, P(v), P(P(v)), \ldots, r$

The first element of the *longest common suffix* of these two sequences is then trivially the lca.

Time complexity of this algorithm is $O(h)$ where h is the height of the tree. For a quite balanced tree, h is $O(\log |V|)$ else it is $O(|V|)$ for a degenerate tree.

3.2.1   C++ Implementation

3.2.1.1   Tree Structure

Program 3.1: Simple n-ary tree

```
 1 #ifndef TREE_HPP
 2 #define TREE_HPP
 3
 4 #include <memory>
 5 #include <iterator>
 6 #include <iostream>
 7
 8 template<typename T>
 9 struct node
10 {
11     node()
12     : parent(0), first_child(0), last_child(0),
13       prev_sibling(0), next_sibling(0) {}
14     node(const T& val)
15     : parent(0), first_child(0), last_child(0),
16       prev_sibling(0), next_sibling(0), data(val)
17     {}
18
19     node<T> *parent;
20     node<T> *first_child, *last_child;
21     node<T> *prev_sibling, *next_sibling;
22     T data;
23 };
24
25 template <typename T, typename Allocator
26                 = std::allocator<node<T>>>
27 struct tree
28 {
29     typedef node<T> tree_node;
30     typedef T value_type;
31
32     tree()
33     {
34         head = alloc_.allocate(1,0);
35         feet = alloc_.allocate(1,0);
36         alloc_.construct(head, node<T>());
37         alloc_.construct(feet, node<T>());
38         head->parent, head->first_child = 0;
39         head->last_child, head->prev_sibling=0;
40         head->next_sibling=feet;
41         feet->parent, feet->first_child = 0;
42         feet->last_child, feet->next_sibling=0;
43         feet->prev_sibling=head;
44     }
45
46     struct iterator
```

```
47      {
48          typedef T   value_type;
49          typedef T*  pointer;
50          typedef T&  reference;
51          typedef size_t size_type;
52          typedef std::ptrdiff_t difference_type;
53          typedef std::bidirectional_iterator_tag
54                      iterator_category;
55
56          iterator() : node(0) {}
57          iterator(tree_node * tn) : node(tn) {}
58
59          T& operator*() const
60          { return node->data; }
61
62          T* operator->() const
63          { return &(node->data); }
64
65          bool operator==(const iterator& o) const
66          {
67              if(o.node==this->node) return true;
68              else return false;
69          }
70          bool operator!=(const iterator& o) const
71          {
72              if(o.node!=this->node) return true;
73              else return false;
74          }
75          tree_node *node;
76      };
77
78      iterator begin() const
79      {
80          return iterator(head->next_sibling);
81      }
82
83      iterator end() const
84      { return iterator(feet); }
85
86      template<typename iter>
87      static iter parent(iter p)
88      {
89          return iter(p.node->parent);
90      }
91
92      template<typename iter>
93      iter append(iter p, const T& x)
94      {
95          tree_node* tmp = alloc_.allocate(1,0);
96          alloc_.construct(tmp, x);
97          tmp->first_child, tmp->last_child=0;
98          tmp->parent=p.node;
99          if(p.node->last_child!=0)
100         {
101             p.node->last_child->next_sibling=tmp;
102         }
103         else
104         {
105             p.node->first_child=tmp;
106         }
107         tmp->prev_sibling=p.node->last_child;
108         p.node->last_child=tmp;
109         tmp->next_sibling=0;
110         return tmp;
111     }
```

```
112
113    static int level(const iterator& it)
114    {
115        tree_node* pos=it.node;
116        int l = 0;
117        while(pos->parent!=0)
118        {
119                pos=pos->parent;
120                ++l;
121        }
122        return l;
123    }
124
125    template<typename iter>
126    iter insert(iter p, const T& x)
127    {
128        if(p.node==0)
129        {
130            p.node=feet;
131        }
132        tree_node* tmp = alloc_.allocate(1,0);
133        alloc_.construct(tmp, x);
134        tmp->first_child, tmp->last_child = 0;
135        tmp->parent=p.node->parent;
136        tmp->next_sibling=p.node;
137        tmp->prev_sibling=p.node->prev_sibling;
138        p.node->prev_sibling=tmp;
139
140        if(tmp->prev_sibling==0)
141        {
142            if(tmp->parent)
143            tmp->parent->first_child=tmp;
144        }
145        else
146        {
147            tmp->prev_sibling->next_sibling=tmp;
148        }
149        return tmp;
150
151    }
152    tree_node *head, *feet;
153 private:
154    Allocator alloc_;
155 };
156
157 #endif
```

3.2.2   Compute LCA : C++ : Stack Based

Program 3.2: Compute LCA : C++ : Stack Based

```
1 #include <iostream>
2 #include <stack>
3 #include "tree.hpp"
4
5 template<typename T>
6 typename tree<T>::iterator
7 lca(const tree<T> & tree,
8      typename tree<T>::iterator u,
9      typename tree<T>::iterator v)
10 {
11    std::stack<typename tree<T>::iterator>
12        s1, s2;
13
14    typename tree<T>::iterator lca;
15
```

```
16      do
17      {
18          s1.push(u);
19          if (u!= tree.begin())
20              u = tree.parent(u);
21      } while (u != tree.begin());
22
23      s1.push(tree.begin());
24
25      do
26      {
27          s2.push(v);
28          if (v!= tree.begin())
29              v = tree.parent(v);
30      } while(v != tree.begin());
31
32      s2.push(tree.begin());
33
34      while(!s1.empty() && !s2.empty()
35          && (s1.top() == s2.top()))
36      {
37          lca = s1.top();
38
39          s1.pop();
40          s2.pop();
41      }
42
43      return lca;
44 }
45
46 int main()
47 {
48      tree<std::string> st;
49      tree<std::string>::iterator itra =
50          st.insert(st.begin(), "a");
51      tree<std::string>::iterator itrb =
52          st.append(itra, "b");
53      tree<std::string>::iterator itrc =
54          st.append(itra, "c");
55
56      tree<std::string>::iterator itrd, itre;
57      itrd = st.append(itrb, "d");
58      itre = st.append(itrb, "e");
59      st.append(itre, "h");
60
61      tree<std::string>::iterator itri =
62          st.append(itre, "i");
63      tree<std::string>::iterator itrm =
64          st.append(itri, "m");
65      tree<std::string>::iterator itrn =
66          st.append(itri, "n");
67      tree<std::string>::iterator itro =
68          st.append(itri, "o");
69
70      tree<std::string>::iterator itrf =
71          st.append(itrd, "f");
72      tree<std::string>::iterator itrg =
73          st.append(itrd, "g");
74      tree<std::string>::iterator itrj =
75          st.append(itrf, "j");
76      tree<std::string>::iterator itrk =
77          st.append(itrf, "k");
78      tree<std::string>::iterator itrl =
79          st.append(itrf, "l");
80
81
82      tree<std::string>::iterator pi, pe, pb;
```

```
83      pi = tree<std::string>::parent(itri);
84      pe = tree<std::string>::parent(pi);
85      pb = tree<std::string>::parent(pe);
86
87   std::cout << "Parent of nodes : "
88        << "\ni :" << *pi
89        << "\ne :" << *pe
90        << "\nb :" << *pb << "\n" << std::endl;
91
92   std::cout << "lca of b and c : "
93        << *lca(st, itrb, itrc) << std::endl;
94   std::cout << "lca of d and e : "
95        << *lca(st, itrd, itre) << std::endl;
96   std::cout << "lca of f and e : "
97        << *lca(st, itrf, itre) << std::endl;
98   std::cout << "lca of f and i : "
99        << *lca(st, itrf, itri) << std::endl;
100  std::cout << "lca of f and g : "
101       << *lca(st, itrf, itrg) << std::endl;
102  std::cout << "lca of j and l : "
103       << *lca(st, itrj, itrl) << std::endl;
104  std::cout << "lca of l and o: "
105       << *lca(st, itrl, itro) << std::endl;
106  std::cout << "lca of b and o : "
107       << *lca(st, itrb, itro) << std::endl;
108  std::cout << "lca of a and a : "
109       << *lca(st, itra, itra) << std::endl;
110  std::cout << "lca of j and c : "
111       << *lca(st, itrj, itrc) << std::endl;
112 }
```

This prints:

```
Parent of nodes :
i :e
e :b
b :a

lca of b and c : a
lca of d and e : b
lca of f and e : b
lca of f and i : b
lca of f and g : d
lca of j and l : f
lca of l and o: b
lca of b and o : b
lca of a and a : a
lca of j and c : a
```

Let us draw the tree again for quick reference:

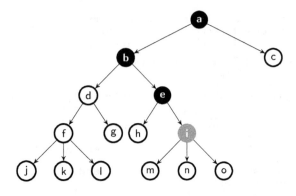

3.2.3   Compute LCA : C++ : Level Based

Program 3.3: Compute LCA : C++ : Level Based

```
1 #include <iostream>
2 #include <stack>
3 #include "tree.hpp"
4
5 template<typename T>
6 typename tree<T>::iterator
7 lca(const tree<T> & tree ,
8       typename tree<T>::iterator u,
9       typename tree<T>::iterator v)
10 {
11      while(tree.level(u) > tree.level(v))
12      {
13          u = tree.parent(u);
14      }
15
16      while(tree.level(v) > tree.level(u))
17      {
18          v = tree.parent(v);
19      }
20
21      while(u != v)
22      {
23          u = tree.parent(u);
24          v = tree.parent(v);
25      }
26
27      return u;
28 }
29
30 int main()
31 {
32      tree<std::string> st;
33      tree<std::string>::iterator itra
34          = st.insert(st.begin(), "a");
35      tree<std::string>::iterator itrb
36          = st.append(itra, "b");
37      tree<std::string>::iterator itrc
38          = st.append(itra, "c");
39
40      tree<std::string>::iterator itrd , itre;
41      itrd = st.append(itrb, "d");
42      itre = st.append(itrb, "e");
43      st.append(itre, "h");
44
45      tree<std::string>::iterator itri
```

```
46        = st.append(itre, "i");
47    tree<std::string>::iterator itrm
48        = st.append(itri, "m");
49    tree<std::string>::iterator itrn
50        = st.append(itri, "n");
51    tree<std::string>::iterator itro
52        = st.append(itri, "o");
53
54    tree<std::string>::iterator itrf
55        = st.append(itrd, "f");
56    tree<std::string>::iterator itrg
57        = st.append(itrd, "g");
58    tree<std::string>::iterator itrj
59        = st.append(itrf, "j");
60    tree<std::string>::iterator itrk
61        = st.append(itrf, "k");
62    tree<std::string>::iterator itrl
63        = st.append(itrf, "l");
64
65
66    std::cout << "levels of nodes \n:"
67        << "\na: " << st.level(itra)
68        << "\nb: " << st.level(itrb)
69        << "\nd: " << st.level(itrd)
70        << "\ne: " << st.level(itre)
71        << "\ni: " << st.level(itri)
72        << "\nf: " << st.level(itrf)
73        << "\n" << std::endl;
74
75    tree<std::string>::iterator pi, pe, pb;
76    pi = tree<std::string>::parent(itri);
77    pe = tree<std::string>::parent(pi);
78    pb = tree<std::string>::parent(pe);
79
80    std::cout << "lca of b and c : "
81        << *lca(st, itrb, itrc) << std::endl;
82    std::cout << "lca of d and e : "
83        << *lca(st, itrd, itre) << std::endl;
84    std::cout << "lca of f and e : "
85        << *lca(st, itrf, itre) << std::endl;
86    std::cout << "lca of f and i : "
87        << *lca(st, itrf, itri) << std::endl;
88    std::cout << "lca of f and g : "
89        << *lca(st, itrf, itrg) << std::endl;
90    std::cout << "lca of j and l : "
91        << *lca(st, itrj, itrl) << std::endl;
92    std::cout << "lca of l and o: "
93        << *lca(st, itrl, itro) << std::endl;
94    std::cout << "lca of b and o : "
95        << *lca(st, itrb, itro) << std::endl;
96    std::cout << "lca of a and a : "
97        << *lca(st, itra, itra) << std::endl;
98    std::cout << "lca of j and c : "
99        << *lca(st, itrj, itrc) << std::endl;
100   std::cout << "lca of d and c : "
101       << *lca(st, itrd, itrc) << std::endl;
102 }
```

This prints:

```
levels of nodes
:
a: 0
b: 1
```

```
d: 2
e: 2
i: 3
f: 3

lca of b and c : a
lca of d and e : b
lca of f and e : b
lca of f and i : b
lca of f and g : d
lca of j and l : f
lca of l and o: b
lca of b and o : b
lca of a and a : a
lca of j and c : a
lca of d and c : a
```

3.3   Constant Time LCA

The LCA problem is then, given a rooted tree T for preprocessing, preprocess it in a way so that the LCA of any two given nodes in T can be retrieved in constant time. Let us present a preprocessing algorithm that requires no more than linear time and space complexity.

We make the following two assumptions on our computational machine model. Let n denote the size of our input in unary representation:

1. All arithmetic, comparative and logical operations on numbers whose binary representation is of size no more then $\log n$ bits can be done in *constant* time.

2. We assume that finding the left-most bit or the right-most bit of a $\log n$ sized number can be done in *constant* time.

3.3.1   Complete Binary Tree

Our discussion begins with a particularly simple instance of the LCA problem, LCA queries on complete binary trees. We will use our knowledge of solving the LCA problem on complete binary trees and expand it later on, to solve the LCA problem on any arbitrary rooted tree T.

Let B denote a complete binary tree with n nodes. The key thing here is to encode the unique path from the root to a node in the node itself. We assign each node a *path number*, a $\log n$ bit number that encodes the unique path from the root to the node.

3.3.1.1   Path Number

For each node v in B we encode a *path number* in the following way:

- Counting from the left most bit, the i'th bit of the path number for v corresponds to the i'th edge on the path from the root to v.

- A **0** for the i'th bit from the left indicates that the i'th edge on the path goes to a left child, and a **1** indicates that it goes to a right child.

- Let k denote then number of edges on the path from the root to v, then we mark the $k+1$ bit (the height bit) of the path number **1**, and the rest of the $\log n - k - 1$ bits **0**.

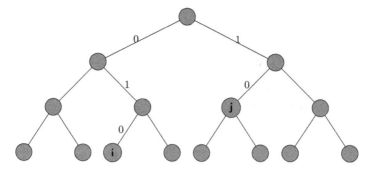

- Node i's path number is

$$0\ 1\ 0\ \mathbf{1}$$

- Node j's path number is

$$\mathbf{1}\ 0\ 1\ \mathit{0}$$

Please note that the height bit is marked in **bold** and padded bits are marked in *italics*.

Path numbers can easily be assigned in a simple $O(n)$ *in-order* traversal on B.

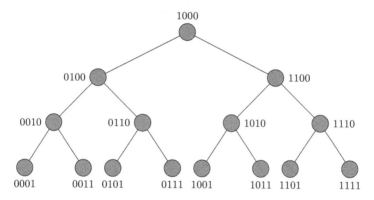

3.3.1.2 LCA Queries in Complete Binary Tree

Suppose now that u and v are two nodes in B, and that *path(u)* and *path(v)* are their appropriate path numbers.

We denote the lowest common ancestor of u and v as *lca(u,v)*.

We denote the prefix bits in the path number, those that correspond to edges on the path from the root, as the *path bits* of the path number.

1. First we calculate *path(u) XOR path(v)* and find the left most bit which equals **1**.

2. If there is no such bit then *path(u)* = *path(v)* and so $u = v$, so assume that the k'th bit of the result is **1**.

3. If both the k'th bit in *path(u)* and the k'th bit in *path(v)* are *path bits*, then this means that u and v agree on *k-1* edges of their path from the root, meaning that the *k-1* prefix of each node's path number encodes within it the path from the root to *lca(u,v)*.

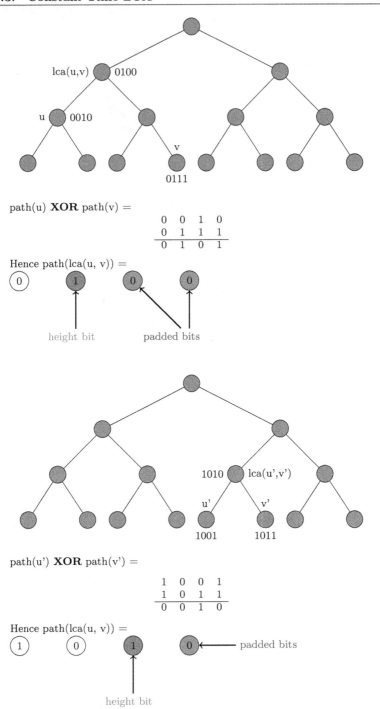

path(u) **XOR** path(v) =

0	0	1	0
0	1	1	1
0	1	0	1

Hence path(lca(u, v)) =

height bit   padded bits

path(u') **XOR** path(v') =

1	0	0	1
1	0	1	1
0	0	1	0

Hence path(lca(u, v)) =

padded bits

height bit

This concludes that if we take the prefix $k - 1$ bits of the result of *path(u) XOR path(v)*, add **1** as the k'th bit, and pad $\log n - k$ **0** suffix bits, we get *path(lca(u,v))*.

If either the k'th bit in *path(u)* or the k'th bit in *path(v)* (or both) is not a path bit then one node is ancestor to the other, and *lca(u,v)* can easily be retrieved by comparing *path(u)* and *path(v)*'s height bit.

3.4   The general LCA algorithm

The following are the two stages of the general *LCA* algorithm for any arbitrary tree T:

1. First, we reduce the *LCA* problem to the *Restricted Range Minima* problem. The *Restricted Range Minima* problem is the problem of finding the smallest number in an interval of a fixed list of numbers, where the difference between two successive numbers in the list is exactly one.

2. Second, we solve the *Restricted Range Minima* problem and thus solve the *LCA* problem.

For more details, please refer [6].

Chapter 4

Max Sub-Array Problem

Problem 4 (*Kadane*)

Design and implement an efficient program to find a contiguous subarray within a one-dimensional array of integers which has the largest sum. Please note that there is at least one positive integer in the input array.

Solution

4.1 Kadane's Algorithm

There is scanning algorithm known as *Kadane's algorithm* which keeps track of the maximum sum subarray by starting at the leftmost element and scanning through to the rightmost element. It works in a dynamic programming set-up because it has an optimal substructure, i.e., the maximum sum subarray upto the $(i-1)^{th}$ element is used to find maximum sum subarray upto i^{th} element.

The algorithm accumulates a partial sum in max_ending_here and updates the current solution max_so_far appropriately. It is increased by the value contained in i^{th} index as far as it keeps it positive, it is reset to zero otherwise.

If all elements of an array are non-negative, this problem is trivial, as the entire array represents the solution. Similarly, if all elements are non-positive, the solution is empty with value 0. So we consider a data set containing both positive and negative values.

Algorithm 14 Kadane's 1D Algorithm

1: **function** KADANE1D(start, end)
2:     $max\_so\_far \leftarrow 0$
3:     $max\_ending\_here \leftarrow 0$
4:     **while** $start \neq end$ **do**
5:         max_ending_here ← max(max_ending_here + *start, 0)
6:         max_so_far ← max(max_so_far, max_ending_here)
7:         start ← start + 1
8:     **end while**
9:     **return** max_so_far
10: **end function**

4.1.1 C++11 Implementation

Program 4.1: Implementing Kadane's Algorithm

```
1 #include <algorithm>
2
3 template <typename ForwardIterator>
4 typename std::iterator_traits<
5     ForwardIterator >::value_type
6 kadane1d(ForwardIterator start,
7          ForwardIterator end)
8 {
9     typedef typename std::iterator_traits<
10        ForwardIterator
11        >::value_type value_type;
12
13    value_type max_so_far = 0,
14               max_ending_here = 0;
15
16    while(start != end)
17    {
18        max_ending_here =
19            std::max(max_ending_here + *start++,
20                0);
21        max_so_far =
22        std::max(max_so_far, max_ending_here);
23    }
24    return max_so_far;
25 }
```

4.1.2 Usage

Program 4.2: Implementing Kadane's Algorithm

```
1 #include <iostream>
2 #include <array>
3 #include <vector>
4 #include <forward_list>
5 #include "kadane1d.hpp"
6
7 int main()
8 {
9     std::array<int, 8> a
10    {-2, -3, 4, -1, -2, 1, 5, -3};
11
12    std::cout << kadane1d(a.cbegin(), a.cend())
13             << std::endl;
14
15    std::vector<int> v
16    {-1, 4, -2, 5, -5, 2, -20, 6};
17
18    std::cout << kadane1d(v.cbegin(), v.cend())
19             << std::endl;
20
21    std::forward_list<int> l
22    {-2, 1, -3, 4, -1, 2, 1, -5, 4};
23
24    std::cout << kadane1d(l.cbegin(), l.cend())
25             << std::endl;
26 }
```

It prints

```
7
7
6
```

4.2 Find indices of max subarray

Design and implement an efficient program to find a contiguous subarray within a one-dimensional array of integers which has the largest sum. The result should include sum and (start, end) of the subarray.

It is easy to see that

- the maximum subarray starts and ends in positive elements
- if we start from the first positive element, i.e., a[l], and sum over the subsequent elements until the sum drops negative at a[r], then the optimal subarray is either
    - in a[l..r] and starts from a[l], or
    - in a[r + 1..n].

Algorithm 15 Kadane's 1D Algorithm : Find Indices

1: **function** KADANE1D(start, end)
2:     $max\_so\_far \leftarrow 0$
3:     $max\_ending\_here \leftarrow 0$
4:     $l \leftarrow 0$
5:     $r \leftarrow 0$
6:     $li \leftarrow 0$
7:     **while** $start \neq end$ **do**
8:         max_ending_here ← (max_ending_here + *start)
9:         **if** max_ending_here < 0 **then**
10:            max_ending_here ← 0
11:            li ←start + 1
12:        **end if**
13:        **if** max_so_far < max_ending_here **then**
14:            max_so_far ← max_ending_here
15:            l ← li
16:            r ← start
17:        **end if**
18:        start ← start + 1
19:     **end while**
20:     **return** <max_so_far, l, r>
21: **end function**

4.2.1 C++11 Implementation

Program 4.3: Implementing Kadane's Algorithm : Finding Indices

```
 1 #include <algorithm>
 2 #include <tuple>
 3
 4 template <typename ForwardIterator>
 5 std :: tuple<typename std :: iterator_traits<
 6                 ForwardIterator
 7                 >:: value_type ,
 8             ForwardIterator , ForwardIterator>
 9 kadane1d ( ForwardIterator start ,
10             ForwardIterator end)
11 {
12     typedef typename std :: iterator_traits<
13                 ForwardIterator
14                 >:: value_type value_type ;
15
```

```
16      int max_so_far = 0, max_ending_here = 0;
17
18      ForwardIterator starti,
19                      sum_start, sum_end = start;
20
21      while(start != end)
22      {
23          max_ending_here += *start;
24
25          if(max_ending_here < 0)
26          {
27              max_ending_here = 0;
28              starti = start;
29              ++starti;
30          }
31
32          if(max_so_far < max_ending_here)
33          {
34              max_so_far = max_ending_here;
35              sum_start = starti;
36              sum_end = start;
37          }
38          ++start;
39      }
40
41      return std::make_tuple(max_so_far,
42                             sum_start,
43                             sum_end);
44 }
```

4.2.2 Usage

In practice, a bitmap image has all non-negative pixel values. When the average is subtracted from each pixel, we can apply the maximum subarray algorithm to find the brightest area within the image.

Program 4.4: Using Kadane's Algorithm : Finding Indices

```
 1 #include <iostream>
 2 #include <forward_list>
 3 #include "kadane1d_indices.hpp"
 4
 5 template<typename ForwardIterator>
 6 void printcontents(ForwardIterator start,
 7                    ForwardIterator end)
 8 {
 9     std::cout << "{";
10     while(start != end)
11     {
12         std::cout << *start++ << " ";
13     }
14     std::cout << *start << "}" << std::endl;
15 }
16
17 int main()
18 {
19     std::tuple<int, int*, int*> sum_start_end;
20
21     std::array<int, 8> a
22     {-2, -3, 4, -1, -2, 1, 5, -3};
23
24     sum_start_end =
25       kadane1d(a.begin(), a.end());
26
27     auto max_sum = std::get<0>(sum_start_end);
28
29     auto start_index =
```

```
30          std :: distance(std :: begin(a) ,
31              std :: get<1>(sum_start_end));
32
33      auto end_index =
34          std :: distance(std :: begin(a) ,
35              std :: get<2>(sum_start_end));
36
37      std :: cout << "<sum : " << max_sum << ","
38          << " start index : " << start_index << ","
39          << " end index : " << end_index << ">"
40          << " \nMax subarray is : ";
41
42      printcontents(std :: get<1>(sum_start_end) ,
43                      std :: get<2>(sum_start_end));
44
45      std :: vector<int> v
46      {−1, 4, −2, 5, −5, 2, −20, 6};
47
48      typedef std :: vector<int >:: iterator vitr ;
49      std :: tuple<int , vitr , vitr >
50        sum_start_end_v;
51
52      sum_start_end_v =
53          kadane1d(v.begin() , v.end());
54
55      max_sum = std :: get<0>(sum_start_end_v);
56
57      start_index =
58        std :: distance(v.begin() ,
59            std :: get<1>(sum_start_end_v));
60
61      end_index = std :: distance(v.begin() ,
62                      std :: get<2>(sum_start_end_v));
63
64      std :: cout << "<sum : " << max_sum << ","
65          << " start index : " << start_index << ","
66          << " end index : " << end_index << ">"
67          << " \nMax subarray is : ";
68
69      printcontents(std :: get<1>(sum_start_end_v) ,
70                      std :: get<2>(sum_start_end_v));
71
72
73      std :: forward_list<int> l
74      {−2, 1, −3, 4, −1, 2, 1, −5, 4};
75
76      typedef std :: forward_list<int >:: iterator
77          litr ;
78      std :: tuple<int , litr , litr > sum_start_end_l;
79
80      sum_start_end_l =
81          kadane1d(l.begin() , l.end());
82
83      max_sum = std :: get<0>(sum_start_end_l);
84
85      start_index = std :: distance(l.begin() ,
86                      std :: get<1>(sum_start_end_l));
87
88      end_index = std :: distance(l.begin() ,
89                      std :: get<2>(sum_start_end_l));
90
91      std :: cout << "<sum : " << max_sum << ","
92          << " start index : " << start_index << ","
93          << " end index : " << end_index << ">"
94          << " \nMax subarray is : ";
95      printcontents(std :: get<1>(sum_start_end_l) ,
96                      std :: get<2>(sum_start_end_l));
97  }
```

It prints

```
<sum : 7, start index : 2, end index : 6>
Max subarray is : {4 -1 -2 1 5}
<sum : 7, start index : 1, end index : 3>
Max subarray is : {4 -2 5}
<sum : 6, start index : 3, end index : 6>
Max subarray is : {4 -1 2 1}
```

4.2.3   Time Complexity

This algorithm consists of n additions and at most 2n comparisons, so the complexity is around 3n.

Hence complexity is linear, i.e., $O(n)$.

4.3   Find subarray with sum closest to zero

Find a sub-array whose sum is closest to zero rather than that with maximum sum. Please note that closest to zero doesn't mean minimum sum

Assuming input array is a, let us have a notion of *prefix array prefixa* such that
$prefixa[i] = a[0] + a[1] + a[2] + \ldots + a[i-1] + a[i]$
$\Longrightarrow$
$prefixa[i] = prefixa[i-1] + a[i]$
$\Longrightarrow$
$a[i] = prefixa[i] - prefixa[i-1]$

Suppose a[l..k] be such a sub-array with sum closest to zero. Then we have the sum of this sub-array as :
$a[l] + a[l+1] + \ldots + a[k-1] + a[k]$
$=$
$prefixa[l] - prefixa[l-1] +$
$prefixa[l+1] - prefixa[l] +$
$\vdots$
$prefixa[k-1] - prefixa[k-2] +$
$prefixa[k] - prefixa[k-1]$
$=$
$prefixa[k] - prefixa[l-1]$

Hence for the sum of a[l..k] to be equal to zero, we should have
$prefixa[k] = prefixa[l-1]$

Hence the sum closest to zero can be found by locating the two closest elements in *prefixa*.

Let us formalize the above algorithm as follows:

1. Compute prefix array with index of original array as well, so it is a collection of pair(value, index). $O(n)$

2. Sort the above prefix array by value. $O(nlogn)$

3. Compute pair-wise diff by value. Prepare absolute values to get a measure of how far/close these are to zero. $O(n)$

4. The closest pair is that with minimum value found above. $O(n)$

5. Report the indices found above in the original array. This is the subarray with sum being closest to zero. (2 comparisons needed).

Please note that the first and last entries of the suffix array are sentinel points(hence special cases) because these cannot be represented effectively by any other two sub prefix sum. Suppose the closest pair indices reported above is (l, k), then the sub-array with sum closest to zero will be decided by the minimum of (closest pair-wise diff val, first entry of prefix, last entry of prefix), i.e. the desired subarray would be

- a[l..k] if closest pair-wise diff val is minimum
- a[0] if first entry of prefix is minimum
- a[0..n - 1] is last entry of prefix is minimum

Hence overall time complexity is $O(n + nlogn)$

Let us start walking through an implementation approach in C++ to understand it better.

Program 4.5: Finding sum closest to zero

```
#include <utility>
#include <algorithm>
#include <tuple>
#include <iostream>

typedef std::pair<int, size_t> ValueIndexPair;

std::vector<int> i
findSubArraySumZero(std::vector<int>& a)
{
    typedef std::tuple<int, size_t, size_t>
        ValStartEndIndices;

    size_t len = a.size();
    std::vector<ValueIndexPair> prefixa(len);

    prefixa[0] = ValueIndexPair(a[0], 0);

    for(size_t i = 1; i < len; ++i)
    prefixa[i] =
    ValueIndexPair(
      prefixa[i - 1].first + a[i], i);

    std::cout <<
    "Printing Prefix Array with Value and"
    " Original Index"
    << std::endl;

    for(ValueIndexPair vip : prefixa)
    std::cout << vip.first << ":"
              << vip.second << " ";
    std::cout << std::endl;

    int start_prefix = prefixa[0].first;
    int end_prefix = prefixa[len - 1].first;

    std::sort(prefixa.begin(), prefixa.end(),
        [](ValueIndexPair f, ValueIndexPair s)
        {
            return f.first < s.first;
        }
    );

    std::cout
    << "Printing Value Sorted Prefix Array"
    << std::endl;

    for(ValueIndexPair vip : prefixa)
    std::cout << vip.first << ":"
              << vip.second << " ";
    std::cout << std::endl;
```

```
52
53   std::vector<ValStartEndIndices>
54       pairwisediff_vec(len - 1);
55   for(size_t i = 0; i < len - 1; ++i)
56   {
57       pairwisediff_vec[i] =
58       std::make_tuple(
59       prefixa[i + 1].first - prefixa[i].first,
60       prefixa[i].second,
61       prefixa[i + 1].second);
62   }
63
64   std::cout <<
65   "Printing Pairwise Value Differences with"
66   " original indices"
67   << std::endl;
68
69   for(ValStartEndIndices vsei :
70       pairwisediff_vec)
71   std::cout << "("
72             << std::get<0>(vsei) << ":"
73             << std::get<1>(vsei) << ":"
74             << std::get<2>(vsei) << ") ";
75   std::cout << std::endl;
76
77   std::vector<ValStartEndIndices>::iterator
78   itr =
79   std::min_element(
80       pairwisediff_vec.begin(),
81       pairwisediff_vec.end(),
82       [](ValStartEndIndices f,
83          ValStartEndIndices s)
84       {
85           return std::abs(std::get<0>(f))
86                  < std::abs(std::get<0>(s));
87       }
88   );
89
90   ValStartEndIndices closest_indices = *itr;
91
92   std::vector<int> vcandidates(3);
93
94   vcandidates[0] =
95    std::abs(std::get<0>(closest_indices));
96   vcandidates[1] =
97    std::abs(start_prefix); // a[0]
98   vcandidates[2] =
99    std::abs(end_prefix); // a[0..n - 1]
100
101  int close_zero = *std::min_element(
102   vcandidates.begin(), vcandidates.end());
103
104  std::vector<int> vsumzero;
105
106  size_t start_index, end_index = 0;
107
108  if(close_zero == vcandidates[1])
109  {
110      vsumzero.push_back(a[0]);
111  }
112  else if(close_zero == vcandidates[2])
113  {
114      vsumzero = a;
115  }
116  else // close_zero == vcandidates[0])
```

```
117     {
118         std::pair<size_t, size_t> se =
119         std::minmax(std::get<1>(
120             closest_indices),
121             std::get<2>(closest_indices));
122
123         vsumzero.assign(a.begin() +
124                         se.first + 1,
125                 a.begin() + se.second + 1);
126     }
127
128     return vsumzero;
129 }
130
131 int main()
132 {
133     std::vector<int> v
134     { 8, -3, 2, 1, -4, 10, -5 };
135
136     std::vector<int> vclosest_sum_zero =
137         findSubArraySumZero(v);
138
139     std::cout << "Subarray with sum closest"
140     "to zero is" << std::endl;
141     for(int e : vclosest_sum_zero)
142     std::cout << e << " ";
143     std::cout << std::endl;
144     std::cout << std::endl;
145
146     v = {-3,2,4,-6,-8,10,11};
147     vclosest_sum_zero = findSubArraySumZero(v);
148
149     std::cout << "Subarray with sum closest to"
150     " zero is" << std::endl;
151     for(int e : vclosest_sum_zero)
152     std::cout << e << " ";
153     std::cout << std::endl;
154     std::cout << std::endl;
155
156     v = {10, -2, -7};
157     vclosest_sum_zero = findSubArraySumZero(v);
158
159     std::cout << "Subarray with sum closest to"
160     " zero is" << std::endl;
161     for(int e : vclosest_sum_zero)
162     std::cout << e << " ";
163     std::cout << std::endl;
164     std::cout << std::endl;
165 }
```

It prints

```
Printing Prefix Array with Value and Original Index
8:0 5:1 7:2 8:3 4:4 14:5 9:6
Printing Value Sorted Prefix Array
4:4 5:1 7:2 8:0 8:3 9:6 14:5
Printing Pairwise Value Differences with
original indices
(1:4:1) (2:1:2) (1:2:0) (0:0:3) (1:3:6) (5:6:5)
Subarray with sum closest to zero is
-3 2 1


Printing Prefix Array with Value and Original Index
```

```
-3:0 -1:1 3:2 -3:3 -11:4 -1:5 10:6
Printing Value Sorted Prefix Array
-11:4 -3:0 -3:3 -1:1 -1:5 3:2 10:6
Printing Pairwise Value Differences with
original indices
(8:4:0) (0:0:3) (2:3:1) (0:1:5) (4:5:2) (7:2:6)
Subarray with sum closest to zero is
2 4 -6

Printing Prefix Array with Value and Original Index
10:0 8:1 1:2
Printing Value Sorted Prefix Array
1:2 8:1 10:0
Printing Pairwise Value Differences with
original indices
(7:2:1) (2:1:0)
Subarray with sum closest to zero is
10 -2 -7
```

4.4 Find subarray with sum closest to k

Find a sub-array whose sum is closest to a integer s.

As can be seen from the previous problem that the sum of a[l..k] = $prefixa[k] - prefixa[l-1] = s$

Hence in order to find the sub-array with sum closest to zero, all we need to find is to locate 2 elements in the prefix array which are closest with respect to k-distance.

Rest of the exercise is left for the reader to work out.

4.5 Maximum 2D subarray problem

Design and implement an efficient program to find a contiguous 2D subarray within a two-dimensional array of integers which has the largest sum.

Bentley has given a nice algorithm based on Kadane's one dimensional algorithm to solve this problem in two-dimensional array thus making it look like Kadane's 2D algorithm.

It applies Kadane's algorithm to every possible row interval, summing over the rows in each interval to produce one dimensional array for Kadane's algorithm to find the optimal column interval. One of the central idea of Bentley's algorithm is the *prefix sum* , which aims to avoid repeating summations when processing subsequent row intervals. The 1D Kadane'e algorithm is run on the elements of each row of the array $(row_1, row_2 \ldots row_m)$ considered as a 1D stream, then, on the sum of each pair of rows $(row_1 + row_2, row_1 + row_3 \ldots row_1 + row_m)$. The solution is given by the maximal sum produced by the 1D Kadane's algorithm on these cases. If x_1 and x_2 are the pointers to the beginning and the end of the maximal sub-stream, and Row_i and Row_j are the two added rows for which the sum is maximal, then the solution is delimited by the rectangle given by the **upper-left** (Row_i, x_1) and the **lower-right** corners (Row_j, x_2). This algorithm can be summarized as below:

1. Compute the *prefix array* in the dimension of length m. This requires $O(mn)$ computations.

2. If the maximum sum sub-array is between Row_i and Row_j, inclusive, then there are $\frac{m(m+1)}{2}$ such pairs.

3. The sum of elements in the array between Row_i and Row_j for a given column is already computed as a part of our prefix sum. So each column sum looks like a single element of a one dimensional array across all columns, i.e., it looks like a one dimensional array with one row and n columns.

4. Apply Kadane's 1D algorithm on such pairs to get the maximum sub-array as described above. Thus total time complexity is $O(m^2 n)$.

Let us formalize the algorithm as follows:

1. Let us denote the input array as $a[0..m, 0..n]$, i.e., it has m rows and n columns. Let a_i denote the ith row of this array.

2. Let us denote i^{th} rowa of the prefix array as $prefixa_i$ which stands for $a_1 + a_2 \ldots a_i$.

3. Please note that $prefixa_i = prefixa_{i-1} + a_i$, where $i \in 1..m$. As described earlier, the computation of prefix array requires mn additions. Hence $a_i = prefixa_i - prefixa_{i-1}$

4. It is easy to see that the sum over the rows 1 and k, i.e. $a[l..k]$ can be computed as $a_l + a_{l+1} \ldots a_{k-1} + a_k =$
$prefixa_l - prefixa_{l-1} +$
$prefixa_{l+1} - prefixa_l +$

$\vdots$

$prefixa_{k-1} - prefixa_{k-2} +$
$prefixa_k - prefixa_{k-1} =$
$prefixa_k - prefixa_{l-1}$
These consists of $\frac{m(m+1)}{2}$ pairs.

5. Kadane's 1D algorithm is applied on $prefixa_k - prefixa_{l-1}$ for each interval [l,k] to find the maximum sum. Thus overall time complexity is $O(m^2 n)$.

We leave the coding exercise in C++ to the reader.

4.6 K-Maximum Sub-array problem

Design and implement an efficient program to find the K subarrays with largest sums. Please note that the maximum subarray problem for a one- or two-dimensional array is to find the array portion that maiximizes the sum of array elements in it.

Let us revisit our prefix array concept as $a[l..k] = prefixa[k] - prefix[l-1]$. To find the maximum sub-array a[l..k], we have to find the indices l and k which maximizes sum of the entries a[l..k]. Let us denote minprefixa[i] as a minimum prefix array for the sub-array $a[0..i-1]$.
max(a[l..k]) = max(prefixa[k] - prefix[l - 1]) = max(prefixa[k] - min(prefix[l - 1]))
= max(prefixa[k] - minprefixa[k]). So to compute the maximum sub-array all we need to do is to accumulate the prefix sums along with maintaining minimum of the preceding prefix sums which could be subtracted from the accumulated prefix sums to get the maximum sum so far.

Algorithm 16 Maximum sub-array sum using prefix array

1: **function** MAXSUBARRAY(a[0..n - 1])
2:     $minprefixsum \leftarrow 0$
3:     $curmaxsum \leftarrow 0$
4:     $prefixa[0] \leftarrow 0$
5:     **for** $i \leftarrow 0, n - 1$ **do**
6:         $prefixa[i] \leftarrow prefixa[i - 1] + a[i]$
7:         $cand \leftarrow prefixa[i] - minprefixsum$
8:         $curmaxsum \leftarrow max(curmaxsum, cand)$
9:         $minprefixsum \leftarrow min(minprefixsum, prefixa[i])$
10:    **end for**
11:    **return** max_so_far
12: **end function**

Based on the above algorithm, we can easily extend it to find K-maximum sub-array in one dimensional case. Instead of having a single variable that safeguards the minimum prefix sum, we maintain a list of K minimum prefix sums, sorted in non-decreasing order. The merged list of two sorted sequences x and y are denoted by merge(x, y).

Algorithm 17 K-Maximum sub-array sum using prefix array

1: **function** KMAXSUMARRAY(a[0..n - 1])
2:     **for** k $\leftarrow 1, K$ **do**
3:         $min[k] \leftarrow \infty$
4:         $M[k] \leftarrow \infty$
5:     **end for**
6:     $sum[0] \leftarrow 0$
7:     $min[1] \leftarrow 0$
8:     $M[1] \leftarrow 0$
9:     **for** i $\leftarrow 1, n$ **do**
10:        $sum[i] \leftarrow sum[i - 1] + a[i]$
11:        **for** k $\leftarrow 1, K$ **do**
12:            $cand[k] \leftarrow sum[i] - min[k]$
13:        **end for**
14:        $M \leftarrow K largest elements of merge(M, cand)$
15:        insert sum[i] into min
16:    **end for**
17: **end function**

As we need to perform n iterations, the total time complexity is $O(Kn)$. When K = 1, this result is comparable to O(n) time of Kadane's algorithm and prefix array.

Chapter 5

Compute Next Higher Number

Problem 5 (*Gries*)

Compute the next higher number of a given integer using the same digits. It is also know as next higher permutation *of a given number.*

Solution

5.1 Basic Analysis

Let us assume that such a permutation exists and n be the number of digits for the array a. Let us take an example to understand this problem closely. Let the input integer sequence be :

```
{1, 2, 3, 5, 4, 2}
```

Here $n = 6$. We observe the following property for index i = 2:

- a[2] = 3 < 5 = a[3], i.e., a[i] < a[i + 1]
- 5, 4, 2 is a non-increasing sequence, i.e., a[i + 1.. n - 1] is non-increasing
- 4 is the smallest value of the sequence 5, 4, 2 which is greater than 3 such that the immediate next values(2) is less than 3. Let us denote this index as j(4), i.e., a[j] = 4 and $a[j + 1..n - 1] \leq a[i]$.
- Hence the next permutation can be achieved by swapping a[i] with a[j]. $\implies$ 1, 2, 4, 5, 3, 2 is a higher permutation than the original sequence.
- Please note that 5, 3, 2 is a non-increasing sequence. Hence the next higher permutation can be achieved by reversing this part to look like 2, 3, 5.
- Hence the next higher permutation is

```
{1, 2, 4, 2, 3, 5}
```

5.2 Algorithm

So, the process to achieve the next higher permutation can be summarized as below:

1. Compute an index i, $0 \le i < n$ such that $a[i+1..n-1]$ is a non-increasing sequence and $a[i] < a[i+1]$.
2. Compute an index j, $i < j < n$ such that $a[j] > a[i]$ and $a[j+1..n-1] \le a[i]$.
3. swap $a[i]$ and $a[j]$. Now a[i + 1, n - 1] is a non-increasing sequence.
4. reverse $a[j+1..n-1]$ to make it an increasing sequence hence as small as possible.

5.3 C++ Implementation

Program 5.1: C++ Implementation : Find the next higher permutation

```cpp
#include <algorithm>
#include <cassert>
#include <vector>

template <typename BidirectionalIterator>
void next_higher_permutation(
            BidirectionalIterator first ,
            BidirectionalIterator last)
{
    BidirectionalIterator i = last;
    if (first == last || first == --i) return;
    while (true)
    {
        BidirectionalIterator i1 = i;
        if (*--i < *i1)
        {
            BidirectionalIterator j = last;
            while (!(*i < *--j)) ;
            std::iter_swap(i, j);
            std::reverse(i1, last);
            return;
        }
    }
}

int main()
{
    int a[] = {1, 2, 3, 5, 4, 2};
    int aref[] = {1, 2, 4, 2, 3, 5};

    next_higher_permutation(
        std::begin(a), std::end(a));

    assert(std::equal(a, a + 6, aref));

    int b[] = {1, 3, 5, 7, 9, 8, 6, 4, 2};
    int bref[] = {1, 3, 5, 8, 2, 4, 6, 7, 9};

    next_higher_permutation(
        std::begin(b), std::end(b));

    assert(std::equal(std::begin(b),
                      std::end(b), bref));

    int c[] = {3, 8, 2, 7, 6};
    int cref[] = {3, 8, 6, 2, 7};
```

```
48    next_higher_permutation(c, c + 5);
49    assert(std::equal(c, c + 5, cref));
50
51    int d[] =
52      {8, 3, 4, 2, 6, 6, 6, 4, 1, 1};
53    int dref[] =
54      {8, 3, 4, 4, 1, 1, 2, 6, 6, 6};
55
56    next_higher_permutation(
57        std::begin(d), std::end(d));
58
59    assert(std::equal(std::begin(d),
60                      std::end(d), dref));
61
62    std::vector<int> v
63      {1,2,3,4,5,6,7,8,4,9,8,7,6,5,4,3,2,1};
64    std::vector<int> vref
65      {1,2,3,4,5,6,7,8,5,1,2,3,4,4,6,7,8,9};
66
67    next_higher_permutation(
68        v.begin(), v.end());
69
70    assert(std::equal(v.begin(), v.end(),
71                      vref.begin()));
72 }
```

5.4   std::next_permutation

The following version(STL) takes a sequence defined by the range
$[first, last)$ and transforms it into the next permutation which is found by assuming that the set of all permutations is lexicographically sorted with respect to
comp. If such a permutation exists, it returns true. Otherwise, it transforms the
sequence into the smallest permutation, that is, the ascendingly sorted one, and
returns false.

Program 5.2: next_permutation

```
 1 template <typename BidirectionalIterator>
 2 bool next_permutation(
 3          BidirectionalIterator first,
 4          BidirectionalIterator last)
 5 {
 6    BidirectionalIterator i = last;
 7    if (first == last || first == --i)
 8        return false;
 9
10    while (true)
11    {
12        BidirectionalIterator i1 = i;
13        if (*--i < *i1)
14        {
15            BidirectionalIterator j = last;
16            while (!(*i < *--j)) ;
17            std::iter_swap(i, j);
18            std::reverse(i1, last);
19            return true;
20        }
21        if (i == first)
22        {
23            std::reverse(first, last);
24            return false;
25        }
26    }
27 }
```

Program 5.3: reversing a sequence

```cpp
1 template <typename BidirectionalIterator>
2 inline void
3 reverse( BidirectionalIterator first ,
4          BidirectionalIterator last ,
5          bidirectional_iterator_tag)
6 {
7     while ( first != last )
8     {
9         if ( first == --last )
10            break;
11        swap(* first , * last );
12        ++first ;
13    }
14 }
15
16 template <typename RandomAccessIterator>
17 inline void
18 reverse( RandomAccessIterator first ,
19          RandomAccessIterator last ,
20          random_access_iterator_tag)
21 {
22     if ( first != last )
23         for (; first < --last ; ++first )
24             swap(* first , * last );
25 }
26
27 template <typename BidirectionalIterator ,
28           typename OutputIterator>
29 inline OutputIterator
30 reverse_copy( BidirectionalIterator first ,
31               BidirectionalIterator last ,
32               OutputIterator result )
33 {
34     for (; first != last ; ++result )
35         * result = *--last ;
36     return result ;
37 }
38
39 template <typename T>
40 typename enable_if<
41     std :: is_move_constructible<T>:: value &&
42     std :: is_move_assignable<T>:: value
43 >:: type
44 swap(T & x, T & y)
45 {
46     T t ( std :: move(x) );
47     x = std :: move(y);
48     y = std :: move(t);
49 }
50
51 template <typename ForwardIterator1 ,
52           typename ForwardIterator2>
53 inline void iter_swap( ForwardIterator1 a,
54                        ForwardIterator2 b)
55 {
56     swap(*a, *b);
57 }
```

Time Complexity is at most (last - first)/2 swaps.

5.5   Compute previous lower number

The previous lower permutation of a given number is defined as the previous lower number comprising of the same digits.

Compute the previous lower number of a given integer using the same digits.

Let the input integer sequence be :

{1, 2, 4, 2, 3, 5}

Here $n = 6$. We observe the following property for index i = 2:

1. a[2] = 4 < 2 = a[3], i.e., a[i] < a[i + 1]
2. 2, 3, 5 is a non-decreasing sequence, i.e., a[i + 1.. n - 1] is non-decreasing
3. 3 is the value of the sequence 2, 3, 5 which is immediately smaller than 4 such that the next values(5) is greater than(or equal to) 4. Let us denote this index as j(4), i.e., a[j] = 3 and a[j + 1..n − 1] ≥ a[i].
4. Hence the next permutation can be achieved by swapping a[i] with a[j] ⟹ 1, 2, 3, 2, 4, 5 is a lower permutation than the original sequence.
5. Please note that 2, 4, 5 is a non-decreasing sequence. Hence the previous lower permutation can be achieved by reversing this part to look like 5, 4, 2.
6. Hence the previous lower permutation is

{1, 2, 3, 5, 4, 2}

So, the process to achieve the previous lower permutation can be summarized as below:

1. Compute an index i, $0 \leq i < n$ such that $a[i + 1..n − 1]$ is a non-decreasing sequence and $a[i] < a[i + 1]$.
2. Compute an index j, $i < j < n$ such that $a[j] < a[i]$ and $a[j+1..n−1] \geq a[i]$.
3. swap $a[i]$ and $a[j]$. Now a[i + 1, n - 1] is a non-decreasing sequence.
4. reverse $a[j + 1..n − 1]$ to make it a decreasing sequence hence to bring to the just previous higher one.

Program 5.4: C++ Implementation of prev_permutation

```
1 template <typename BidirectionalIterator>
2 bool prev_permutation(
3            BidirectionalIterator  first ,
4            BidirectionalIterator  last )
5 {
6        BidirectionalIterator  i = last ;
7
8        if (first == last || first == −−i )
9            return false ;
10
11       while (true)
12       {
13            BidirectionalIterator  i1 = i ;
14            if (∗i1 < ∗−−i )
15            {
16                 BidirectionalIterator  j = last ;
17                 while (!(∗−−j < ∗i )) ;
18                 std :: iter_swap(i , j );
```

```
19              std :: reverse ( i1 ,  last ) ;
20              return true ;
21          }
22          if  ( i  ==  first )
23          {
24              std :: reverse ( first ,  last ) ;
25              return false ;
26          }
27      }
28 }
```

Program 5.5: Usage of previous permutation

```
1 #include <algorithm>
2 #include <cassert>
3 #include <vector>
4
5 int  main ()
6 {
7      int  aref [] = {1,  2,  3,  5,  4,  2};
8      int  a [] = {1,  2,  4,  2,  3,  5};
9
10     std :: prev_permutation ( std :: begin ( a ) ,
11                                 std :: end ( a ) ) ;
12
13     assert ( std :: equal ( a ,  a + 6 ,  aref ) ) ;
14
15     int  bref [] = {1,  3,  5,  7,  9,  8,  6,  4,  2};
16     int  b [] = {1,  3,  5,  8,  2,  4,  6,  7,  9};
17
18     std :: prev_permutation ( std :: begin ( b ) ,
19                                 std :: end ( b ) ) ;
20
21     assert ( std :: equal ( std :: begin ( b ) ,  std :: end ( b ) ,
22                                 bref ) ) ;
23
24     int  cref [] = {3,  8,  2,  7,  6};
25     int  c [] = {3,  8,  6,  2,  7};
26
27     std :: prev_permutation ( c ,  c + 5 ) ;
28     assert ( std :: equal ( c ,  c + 5 ,  cref ) ) ;
29
30     int  dref [] = {8,  3,  4,  2,  6,  6,  6,  4,  1,  1};
31     int  d [] = {8,  3,  4,  4,  1,  1,  2,  6,  6,  6};
32
33     std :: prev_permutation ( std :: begin ( d ) ,
34                                 std :: end ( d ) ) ;
35
36     assert ( std :: equal ( std :: begin ( d ) ,  std :: end ( d ) ,
37                                 dref ) ) ;
38
39     std :: vector<int> vref
40     {1,2,3,4,5,6,7,8,4,9,8,7,6,5,4,3,2,1};
41     std :: vector<int> v
42     {1,2,3,4,5,6,7,8,5,1,2,3,4,4,6,7,8,9};
43
44     std :: prev_permutation ( v. begin () ,  v.end () ) ;
45
46     assert ( std :: equal ( v. begin () ,  v.end () ,
47                                 vref. begin () ) ) ;
48 }
```

Time Complexity is at most (last - first)/2 swaps.

Chapter 6

2D Binary Search

Let us revisit saddleback search algorithm discussed earlier, where we assumed that the array(or matrix) is *strictly* increasing in both dimensions from a different perspective. For same of simplicity, let us assume that this array consists of natural numbers only. Let us re-instate the problem for quick reference and attention.

Problem 6 (*Gries*)

*Design an efficient algorithm to search for a given integer x in a 2-dimensional **sorted** array a[0..m][0..n]. Please note that it is sorted row-wise and column-wise in ascending order. In case of multiple occurrences, find the list of all pairs(i, j) satisfying a[i, j] == x.*

Solution

6.1 Basic Analysis

It may sound an easy problem to start with. Since array a is a collection of natural numbers and is strictly increasing in each dimension(i.e. sorted both row-wise and column-wise), we can safely infer that

$$a[i, j] == x \implies i \leq x \text{ and } j \leq x$$

Brute force search may involve searching for all possible pairs of values having quadratic complexity involving $(x+1)^2$ comparisons. The search space is confined to a square of size of x + 1 and starting at (0, 0) where it represents top leftmost corner.

Algorithm 18 Exhaustive Search Algorithm

1: **function** EXHAUSTIVE-SEARCH(a[0..x, 0..x], x)
2:    **for** $i \in [0..x]$ **do**
3:       **for** $j \in [0..x]$ **do**
4:          **if** a[i, j] == x **then**
5:             *report the occurrence*
6:          **end if**
7:       **end for**
8:    **end for**
9: **end function**

But as mentioned, we would like to optimize it to reduce the number of comparisons as much as possible. Well, we can reduce the number of comparisons by a factor of two by keeping the search confined to entries lying on or below the diagonal of the rectangular region because $a[i,j] \geq i + j$.

Algorithm 19 Exhaustive Search Algorithm : Improved

1: **function** EXHAUSTIVE-SEARCH(a[0..x, 0..x], x)
2:    **for** $i \in [0..x]$ **do**
3:       **for** $j \in [0..x - i]$ **do**
4:          **if** a[i, j] == x **then**
5:             *report the occurrence*
6:          **end if**
7:       **end for**
8:    **end for**
9: **end function**

Termination condition can be achieved when $x < a[0,0]$ provided we replace

- $[0..x]$ by $[0..x - a[0,0]]$ and
- $[0..x - i]$ by $[0..x - i - a[0,0]]$.

6.2 1D Binary Search

Let us quickly revisit *binary search in one dimensional array*. Fortunately C++ standard library provides an algorithm, namely, *std::binary_ search* which is as follows:

Program 6.1: Implementation of C++ Binary Search

```
template <typename ForwardIterator,
          typename ValueType,
          typename Compare>
inline bool
binary_search(ForwardIterator first,
              ForwardIterator last,
              const ValueType & value,
              Compare comp)
{
    first = std::lower_bound(first, last,
                             value, comp);

    return (first != last) &&
           !comp(value, *first);
}
```

As can be seen that this version doesn't return the position of the element being searched rather it returns a boolean instead which is true if found, false otherwise.

Let us look closely what *std::lower_ bound* is doing which is supposed to return an iterator pointing to the first element in the range [first, last) that is not *less than* value using the compare function.

Program 6.2: Implementation of C++ Lower Bound

```
template <typename ForwardIterator,
          typename ValueType,
          typename Compare>
ForwardIterator
lower_bound(ForwardIterator first,
```

```
6          ForwardIterator last,
7          const ValueType & value,
8          Compare comp)
9  {
10      typedef typename std::iterator_traits<
11              ForwardIterator
12          >::difference_type difference_type;
13
14      difference_type len =
15          std::distance(first, last);
16
17      while (len != 0)
18      {
19          difference_type mid = len / 2;
20          ForwardIterator cur = first;
21
22          std::advance(cur, mid);
23
24          if (comp(*cur, value))
25          {
26              first = ++cur;
27              len -= mid + 1;
28          }
29          else
30              len = mid;
31      }
32      return first;
33 }
```

Let us roll out our own implementation of binary search which will combine these to return a pair(boolean, position) where boolean is true if found in which case position will represent the actual location of element in array, else if boolean is false then position will represent a location within the array where the element being searched can be inserted without violating the ordering(same as lower_bound).

Program 6.3: Custom Implementation of Binary Search

```
1 #include <algorithm>
2
3 template <
4      typename ForwardIterator,
5      typename ValueType,
6      typename Compare = std::less<ValueType>
7 >
8 std::pair<bool, ForwardIterator>
9 binary_search(ForwardIterator first,
10              ForwardIterator last,
11              const ValueType & value,
12              Compare comp = Compare())
13 {
14      first = std::lower_bound(first, last,
15                               value, comp);
16
17      bool found =
18          (first != last && !comp(value, *first));
19
20      return std::pair<bool, ForwardIterator>
21              (found, first);
22 }
```

Program 6.4: Usage of Custom Implementation of Binary Search

```
1 #include <iostream>
2 #include "binary_search.hpp"
3
4 int main()
```

```
5 {
6     int a[] = {2, 6, 8, 13, 20};
7
8     std::pair<bool, int*> res =
9     binary_search(std::begin(a),
10                   std::end(a), 8);
11
12     if(res.first)
13     {
14         std::cout << "8 is found at index : "
15         << std::distance(std::begin(a),
16                          res.second)
17         << std::endl;
18     }
19     else
20     {
21         std::cout << "8 is not found"
22                   << std::endl;
23     }
24 }
```

It prints :

```
8 is found at index : 2
```

All right ! After this quick refresher, let us try using this to solve our original problem of finding an element in a sorted matrix with m rows and n columns, which is a 2D space.

How about applying 1D binary search to each row in succession because each row is sorted ? Complexity of each binary search would be $O(\log n)$. Overall complexity would be $O(m \log n)$.

If we apply 1D binary search to each column in succession instead then its complexity would be $O(n \log m)$.

This is not good enough, because we already have *Saddleback Search Algorithm* with complexity $O(m + n)$ and the basic idea is to improve it further if possible and that too utilizing some sort of two dimensional analogue of binary search. Let us redraw our 2D array :

Astute reader will notice the following facts about this structure:

- a_{11} is the smallest element in the first row as well as in first column $\implies$ it is smallest in the whole matrix.
- a_{mn} is the largest element in the last row as well as in last column $\implies$ it is largest in the whole matrix.
- $a_{22} > a_{12} > a_{11} \implies a_{22} > a_{11}$

- $a_{22} > a_{21} > a_{11} \implies a_{22} > a_{11}$

These observations lead us to think that searching may proceed in phases on some submatrices of reduced sizes, thus discarding those submatrices which doesn't contain the element we are searching for. Now this sounds like 2D analogue of binary search, dubbed as **2D Binary Search** by us.

6.3   Row Based 2D Binary Search

we assume that A is an $m \times n$ sorted matrix, $4 \leq m \leq n$, and x the element to be searched for. When $m < 4$, we can simply apply the naive algorithm searching rows one by one till we reach the optimum.

The basic idea behind this algorithm is the following: Searching proceeds in phases on some sub-matrices with reduced sizes, where in each phase a maximal number of elements which cannot be candidates for x are discarded.

We lay A in the Cartesian plane and let $A(0,0)$ (the smallest) be at the southwest corner and $A(m-1n-1)$ (the largest) at the northeast corner. The row based algorithm works by repeatedly searching for a pivot element on the middle row of A which splits A into sub-matrices. The algorithm is given as the following process and runs by call to $Row - Based - 2D - Binary - Search(A(0..m-1, 0..n-1), x)$

Algorithm 20 Row Based 2D Binary Search

1: **function** ROW-BASED-2D-BINARY-SEARCH(A(r..r', c..c', x)
2:          ▷ Search for x's occurence in $m \times n$ sorted matrix A(r..r', c..c'
3:    $m \leftarrow r' - r$
4:    $n \leftarrow c' - c$
5:    **if** $(m < 4) \lor (n < 4)$ **then**
6:          Use Binary Search on rows/columns and **exit**
7:    **end if**
8:    Use Binary Search to find a pivot element $A(r_{mid}, j)$ on the middle row indexed $r_{mid} = r + \frac{m}{2}$ such that $A(r_{mid}, j) \leq x \leq A(r_{mid}, j+1)$
9:    **if** $(x == A(r_{mid}, j)) \lor (x == A(r_{mid}, j+1))$ **then**
10:          **x** is found and **exit**
11:    **end if**
12:    **if** $x < A(r_{mid}, c)$ **then**
13:          ROW-BASED-2D-BINARY-SEARCH$(A(r_{mid} + 1..r', c..c'), x)$
14:    **else if** $x > A(r_{mid}, c')$ **then**
15:          ROW-BASED-2D-BINARY-SEARCH$(A(r_{mid} + 1..r', c..c'), x)$
16:    **else**
17:          ROW-BASED-2D-BINARY-SEARCH$(A(r_{mid} + 1..r, c..j), x)$
18:          ROW-BASED-2D-BINARY-SEARCH$(A(r..r_{mid}, j + 1..c'), x)$
19:    **end if**
20:                    ▷ Search in A_{NW} and A_{SE} sub-matrices of reduced size
21: **end function**

In each phase of the recursion, the matrix A is divided into 4 sub-matrices according to the pivot element found during the steps in line $12 \ldots 16$:
1. $A_{SW} = A(r..r_{mid}, c..j)$
2. $A_{NW} = A(r_{mid} + 1..r, c..j)$
3. $A_{NE} = A(r_{mid} + 1..r', j + 1..c')$
4. $A_{SE} = A(r..r_{mid}, j + 1..c')$

It is evident that
- $x \notin A_{SW}$ if $x > A(r_{mid}, j)$, and
- $x \notin A_{NE}$ if $x < A(r_{mid}, j+1)$

6.3.1 Time Complexity

Let $T(m, n)$ be the time complexity for searching x in A. It is clear that the algorithm decomposes $T(m, n)$ into *three* parts required for

1. Finding $A(m/2, j)$
2. Searching in A_{NW}
3. Searching in A_{SE}

So, the recurrence relation looks like

$$T(1, n) = O(\log n)$$
$$T(m, 1) = O(\log m)$$
$$T(m, n) = T(m/2, j) + T(m/2, n - j) + O(\log n)$$

It is easy to verify that $T(m, n)$ is maximized when $A_{NW} == A_{SE}$, i.e., $j = n/2$. In this case A is halved in both dimensions in each phase of recursion, so at the end there are m remaining sub-matrices, all with dimension $1 \times n/m$, to be searched.

$$\implies T(m, n) = O(2m \log(2n/m) - \log(n/4)) = O(m \log(2n/m))$$

6.4 Diagonal Based 2D Binary Search

This algorithm splits A in each phase via searching for a pivot on the main diagonal of the middle $m \times m$ sub-matrix, rather than on the middle row of A. The *main diagonal* of a matrix is drawn from its southwest corner to northeast corner. We leave the details to be worked out as an exercise to the reader.

Chapter 7

String Edit Distance

Problem 7 (*Levenshtein*)

Given two strings and a set of edit operations, design and implement an algorithm to minimize the number of edit operations needed to transform the first string into the second. Please note that matches are not counted.

Solution

7.1 Introduction

Finding the occurrences of a given query string (pattern) from a possibly very large text is an old and fundamental problem in computer science. It emerges in applications ranging from text processing and music retrieval to bioinformatics. This task, collectively known as *string matching*, has several different variations. The most natural and simple of these is *exact string matching*, in which, like the name suggests, one wishes to find only occurrences that are exactly identical to the pattern string. This type of search, however, may not be adequate in all applications if for example the pattern string or the text may contain typographical errors. Perhaps the most important applications of this kind arise in the field of bioinformatics, as small variations are fairly common in DNA or protein sequences.

Other related areas of applications include(but not limited to)
- stochastic transduction
- syntactic pattern recognition
- spelling correction
- string correction
- string similarity
- string classification
- pronunciation modeling
- Switchboard corpus
- string permutations

The field of approximate string matching, which has been a research subject since the 1960's, answers the problem of small variation by permitting some error between the pattern and its occurrences. Given an error threshold and a metric to measure the distance between two strings, the task of approximate string matching is to find all substrings of the text that are within (a distance of) the error threshold from the pattern.

7.2   Edit Distance

In this solution we concentrate on approximate string matching that uses so called *unit-cost edit distance* as the metric to measure the distance between two strings. *Edit Distance* between the string S_1 and S_2 is defined in general as the minimal cost of any sequence of edit operations that transforms S_1 into S_2 or vice verse.

There are various types of edit distance metrics available:

- *Levenshtein edit distance* : The allowed edit operations are

  1. insertion,
  2. deletion or
  3. substitution

  of a single character, and each operation has the cost 1. This type of edit distance is sometimes called *unit-cost edit distance*. *Levenshtein edit distance* is perhaps the most common form of edit distance, and often the term edit distance is assimilated to it.

- *Damerau edit distance* : Otherwise identical to the *Levenshtein edit distance*, but allows also the fourth operation of transposing two adjacent characters. A further condition is that the transposed characters must be adjacent before and after the edit operations are applied.

- *Weighted/generalized edit distance* : Allows the same operations as the Levenshtein/Damerau edit distance, respectively, but each operation may have an arbitrary cost.

- *Hamming distance* : Allows only the operation of substituting a character, and each substitution has the unit cost.

- *Longest common subsequence* : Measures the similarity between S_1 and S_2 by the length of their longest common subsequence. This is in effect equivalent to allowing the edit operations of deleting or inserting a single character with the unit cost.

For the sake of simplicity, we will consider two different kinds of edit distances:

1. *Levenshtein edit distance* and
2. *Damerau edit distance*.

These two, and especially the *Levenshtein edit distance*, are the most commonly used forms of unit-cost edit distance.

7.2.1   Levenshtein edit distance

The unit-cost *Levenshtein edit distance* between the strings S_1 and S_2 can be defined as the minimum number of single-character insertions, deletions and substitutions needed in transforming S_1 into S_2 or vice versa.

For example, if $S_1 =$ "cat" and $S_2 =$ "act", then there are two ways to transform S_1 into S_2 with exactly two operations:

1. either

   a) delete $S_1[1] =$ 'c', i.e., "cat" $\Longrightarrow$ "at"

   b) insert a 'c' between the present $S_1[1] =$ 'a' and $S_1[2] =$ 't', i.e., "at" $\Longrightarrow$ "act"

2. or,

   a) substitute $S_1[1] =$ 'c' with an 'a', i.e., "cat" $\Longrightarrow$ "aat"

   b) and substitute the present $S_1[2] =$ 'a' with a 'c', i.e., "aat" $\Longrightarrow$ "act"

So, in either case, *Levenshtein edit distance(S_1, S_2)* is *2*.

7.2.2 Damerau edit distance

In similar fashion, the unit-cost *Damerau edit distance* can be defined as the minimum number of single-character insertions, deletions or substitutions or transpositions between two permanently adjacent characters that are needed in transforming S_1 into S_2 or vice versa.

Continuing with the same example of strings S_1 = "cat" and S_2 = "act", we have that *Damerau edit distance*$(S_1, S_2) = 1$ as now a single transposition of the characters $S_1[0]$= 'c' and $S_1[1]$ = 'a' is enough to convert S_1 into S_2, i.e.

$$\text{transpose "ca" : "cat"} \implies \text{"act"}$$

7.3 Dynamic Programming

Both the *Levenshtein* and the *Damerau edit distance* suit well the technique of dynamic programming. We begin by discussing the dynamic programming algorithm for the *Levenshtein edit distance*.

Let $D(i,j)$ be the edit distance of the strings $S_1[1..i]$ and $S_2[1..j]$, i.e., $D(i,j)$ denotes the minimum number of edit operations needed to transform the first i characters of S_1 into the first j characters of S_2.

If S_1 has m characters and S_2 has n characters, then the edit distance is $D(m,n)$.

7.3.1 Recurrence : Computing the Levenshtein edit distance

We will compute $D(m,n)$ by solving the more general problem of computing $D(i,j)$ for all combinations of i and j, where i ranges from *0* to m and j ranges from *0* to n.

The base conditions are :

- $D(i,0) = i$, i.e., the only way to transform the first i characters of S_1 to *0* characters of S_2 is to *delete* all the i characters of S_1.
- $D(0,j) = j$, i.e., the only way to transform the *0* characters of S_1 to the first j characters of S_2 is to *insert* the j characters of S_2 into S_1.

Then $D(i,j)$ is the minimum of the following three possibilities:

1. $D(i-1,j-1) + \delta(i,j)$, where $\delta(i,j)$ is the cost associated with either substitution(unit cost) or matching(zero cost), i.e.,

    a) $\delta(i,j) = 1$ if $S_1[i] \neq S_2[j]$

    b) $\delta(i,j) = 0$ if $S_1[i] == S_2[j]$

2. $D(i,j-1) + 1$, i.e., *deletion* cost of the character $S_2[j]$
3. $D(i-1,j) + 1$, i.e., *deletion* cost of the character $S_1[i]$

7.3.1.1 C++ Implementation

Program 7.1: Simple Implementation : Levenshtein edit distance

```
1 #include <vector>
2 #include <algorithm>
3 #include <cassert>
4
5 size_t edit_distance (const std :: string & s1 ,
6                       const std :: string & s2 )
7 {
8     const size_t len1 = s1 . size () ,
```

```
9              len2 = s2.size();
10
11    std::vector<std::vector<size_t> >
12        d(len1 + 1,
13          std::vector<size_t>(len2 + 1));
14
15    d[0][0] = 0;
16
17    for(size_t i = 1; i <= len1; ++i)
18    {
19        d[i][0] = i;
20    }
21
22    for(size_t j = 1; j <= len2; ++j)
23    {
24        d[0][j] = j;
25    }
26
27    for(size_t i = 1; i <= len1; ++i)
28        for(size_t j = 1; j <= len2; ++j)
29        {
30            d[i][j] =
31              std::min(
32                      std::min(
33                        d[i - 1][j] + 1,
34                        d[i][j - 1] + 1
35                      ),
36                      d[i - 1][j - 1] +
37                      (s1[i - 1] == s2[j - 1]
38                       ? 0 : 1)
39                      );
40        }
41    return d[len1][len2];
42 }
43
44 int main()
45 {
46    assert(edit_distance("cat", "act") == 2);
47    assert(edit_distance("combo", "coin")
48                                == 3);
49 }
```

Program 7.2: Improved Implementation : Levenshtein edit distance

```
1 #include <vector>
2 #include <algorithm>
3 #include <cassert>
4
5 size_t levenshtein_distance(
6            const std::string &s1,
7            const std::string & s2)
8 {
9    const size_t len1 = s1.size(),
10                 len2 = s2.size();
11
12    std::vector<size_t> col(len2 + 1),
13                        prevCol(len2 + 1);
14
15    for(size_t i = 0; i < prevCol.size(); i++)
16                prevCol[i] = i;
17
18    for (size_t i = 0; i < len1; i++)
19    {
20        col[0] = i+1;
```

```
21
22          for (size_t j = 0; j < len2; j++)
23          {
24              col[j+1] =
25                std::min(
26                  std::min(
27                    1 + col[j],
28                    1 + prevCol[1 + j]
29                  ),
30                  prevCol[j] + (s1[i]==s2[j]
31                  ? 0 : 1)
32                );
33          }
34          col.swap(prevCol);
35      }
36      return prevCol[len2];
37  }
38
39  int main()
40  {
41      assert(levenshtein_distance(
42              "cat", "act") == 2);
43
44      assert(levenshtein_distance(
45              "COMBO", "COIN") == 3);
46  }
```

Program 7.3: Boost Implementation : Levenshtein edit distance

```
1  #include <boost/numeric/ublas/matrix.hpp>
2
3  int levenshtein_distance(
4          const std::string & s1,
5          const std::string & s2)
6  {
7      const size_t len1 = s1.length(),
8                   len2 = s2.length();
9
10     boost::numeric::ublas::matrix<size_t> m(
11         len1 + 1, len2 + 1);
12
13     for(size_t i = 0; i< len1 + 1; ++i)
14     {
15         m(i, 0) = i;
16     }
17
18     for(size_t j = 0; j < len2 + 1; ++j)
19     {
20         m(0, j) = j;
21     }
22
23     size_t cost, cell_cost, min_cost = 0;
24
25     for(size_t i = 0; i < len1; ++i)
26     {
27         cost = 0;
28
29         for(size_t j = 0; j < len2; ++j)
30         {
31             cell_cost = 1;
32
33             if(s2[j] == s1[i])
34             {
35                 cell_cost = 0;
```

```
36              }
37
38              min_cost = m( i ,  j ) ;
39
40              if ( min_cost > m( i ,  j + 1))
41                      min_cost = m( i ,  j + 1) ;
42
43              if ( min_cost > m( i + 1,  j ))
44                      min_cost = m( i + 1,  j ) ;
45
46              cell_cost += min_cost ;
47
48              m( i + 1,  j + 1) = cell_cost ;
49
50              if ( j == 0)
51                      cost = cell_cost ;
52              else
53              {
54                      if ( cell_cost < cost )
55                              cost = cell_cost ;
56              }
57          }
58      }
59      return m( len1 ,  len2 ) ;
60 }
61
62 int  main ()
63 {
64      assert ( levenshtein_distance (
65                      "cat", "act") == 2) ;
66
67      assert ( levenshtein_distance (
68                      "combo", "coin") == 3) ;
69 }
```

7.3.2   Time Complexity

For the computation of $D(i,j)$, we examine only the cells $D(i-1,j-1)$, $D(i,j-1)$ and $D(i-1,j)$, along with the 2 characters $S_1[i]$ and $S_2[j]$. Hence, to fill in one cell takes a constant number of cell examinations, arithmetic operations and comparisons. Because there are $m \times n$ cells in the table computed above, so total time complexity of $D(m,n)$ is $O(mn)$.

7.3.3   Recurrence : Computing the Damerau edit distance

- $D(i,0) = i$
- $D(0,j) = j$

Then $D(i,j)$ is one of the following three possibilities:

1. $D(i-1,j-1)$ if $S_1[i] == S_2[j]$
2. $1 + min(D(i-2,j-2), D(i-1,j), D(i,j-1))$ if $S_1[i-1..i] == reverse(S_2[j-1..j])$
3. $1 + min(D(i-1,j-1), D(i-1,j), D(i,j-1))$ otherwise.

We leave the implementation of this algorithm as an exercise to the reader.

7.3.4   Space Optimization

These basic dynamic programming algorithms clearly have a run time and space consumption of $O(mn)$, as they fill $O(mn)$ cells and filling a single cell takes a constant number of operations and space. It is simple to diminish the needed space into $O(m)$ when column-wise filling order of D is used: When column j is filled, only the cell values in one or two previous columns are needed, depending on whether the *Levenshtein* or the *Damerau distance* is used. This means that it is enough to have only column ($j1$) or also column ($j2$) in memory when computing column j, and so the needed space is $O(m)$.

7.3.5   Properties

It is straightforward to verify that the following properties hold for both the edit distance computation and approximate string matching versions of D under both the *Levenshtein* and the *Damerau* edit distance:

- *Diagonal Property* : $D(i, j)D(i1, j1) = 0$ or 1
- *Adjacency Property* :
  - $D(i, j)D(i, j1) = 1, 0,$ or 1 and
  - $D(i, j)D(i1, j) = 1, 0,$ or 1

7.4   Reduction to Single Source Shortest Path Problem

The solution given by dynamic programming approach involves constructing a table of size $m \times n$, where each entry correspond to a *partial edit* and the goal is to compute the *rightmost bottom* entry, i.e., $D(m, n)$, of the table.

Another way to look at the problem is to consider each entry of the table as a vertex of a directed graph. Thus a vertex corresponds to a *partial* edit. There is an edge (i, j) if the partial edit corresponding to j involves one more edit operation than the partial edit corresponding to i. A simplified directed graph may depict insertions as horizontal edges, deletions as vertical edges and substitutions(or replacements) as diagonal edges.

Hence the string edit distance problem is reduced to a single source shortest path problem as finding a shortest path from the vertex $(0, 0)$ to the vertex (m, n). We leave the implementation details as an exercise to the reader.

Chapter 8

Searching in Two Dimensional Sequence

Problem 8 (*Gries*)

*Design and implement an algorithm to search for a given integer x in a
2-dimensional array a[0..m][0..n] where $0 < m$ and $0 < n$. In case of multiple
occurrences, it doesn't matter which is found.*

Solution

8.1 Basic Analysis

The algorithm should find the position of a given integer x in the array a, i.e.,
the algorithm should find i and j such that

- $\boxed{x = a[i, j]}$, or
- $\boxed{i = m}$

Let us treat the input array as some kind of a rectangular region.

The problem demands that the integer x does exist somewhere in this region. Let
us label this condition as *Input Assertion* or *Precondition*.

8.1.1 Precondition (aka *Input Assertion*)

$$\boxed{x \in a[0..m-1, 0..n-1]}$$

i.e., x is present somewhere in this rectangular region a.

After the program terminates successfully, x has to be found in a rectangular region of a where the rectangular region consists of just one row and column. Let us label this condition as *Output Assertion* or *Result Assertion* or *Postcondition*.

8.1.2   Postcondition (aka *Result Assertion*)

After the program terminates successfully, then x is in a rectangular region of a where the rectangular region consists of just one row and column, i.e., x is present at i^{th} row and j^{th} column of a, or if this is not possible then i = m, i.e., if x is not found in the array, i.e., if $x \neq a[i,j]$, then i = m.

So the Postcondition looks like

$$(0 \leq i \leq m - 1 \wedge 0 \leq j \leq n - 1 \wedge x = a[i,j]) \vee (i = m \wedge x \notin a)$$

Is the search space confined to a rectangular region ?

8.1.3   Invariant

Looking at the precondition and postcondition, it is not that difficult to figure out that during the execution of our algorithm, x is guaranteed to be confined within some L-shaped region of a.

Let us revisit this in light of the invariant which bears that x is not in the already-searched rows a[0..i - 1] and not in the already-searched columns a[i, 0..j - 1] of the current row i.

Let us represent this invariant below:

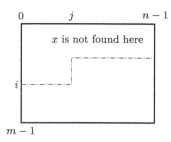

Search space is bounded by L-shaped region

Doesn't it look more like a L-shaped region ?

 Invariant :

$$0 \leq m \wedge 0 \leq j < n \quad \wedge$$

searcheable-region is bounded by $(m - i) * n - j$

Initialization

Before we develop body of the program, let us re-think about what should be the starting point of search, i.e., what should be the initial values of the counters i and j ?

Let us say it is set to 0 to start with, i.e., $i = 0$ and $j = 0$. If this is so then the region marked as **x is not found here** is empty to start with. Fair enough. Invariant still holds true.

8.1.4   Deducing Conditional Statement

Let us start with finding complement of the condition, i.e., search still continues. It is not that difficult to see that this complement should maintain the invariant and lead towards the result, i.e.,

$Invariant \wedge complement - of - condition \implies Postcondition$

8.1.5   Revisiting Postcondition

$(0 \leq i \leq m - 1 \wedge 0 \leq j \leq n - 1 \wedge x = a[i,j]) \vee (i = m \wedge x \notin a)$

As could be seen above, *Postcondition* consists of 2 parts[1]:

1. $(0 \leq i \leq m - 1 \wedge 0 \leq j \leq n - 1 \wedge x = a[i,j])$

2. $(i = m \wedge x \notin a)$

8.1.6   Establishing Postcondition

To establish first part of postcondition, the complement of the condition can be $i < m$ and $x == a[i, j]$.

And to establish second part of postcondition, it can be $i == m$.

---

[1] i.e. 2 disjunctions

8.1.7   Complement of condition

Putting together, this looks like :

$$\boxed{i == m \lor (i < m \text{ and } x == a[i,j])}$$

Let us take its complement again to reach to the condition, i.e., complement of the complement of the condition $\implies$ condition.

8.1.8   Condition

$$\boxed{i \neq m \land (i \geq m \text{ or } x \neq a[i,j])}$$

But this condition has to be evaluated only when the variant is true, i.e., only when $i \leq m$, because as discussed above

$$\boxed{Invariant \land complement - of - condition \implies Postcondition}.$$

So the condition can be simplified further to look like

$$\boxed{i \neq m \land (i == m \text{ or } x \neq a[i,j])}$$

Now, we can safely drop the part $i == m$ because it is already covered by $i \neq m$, so the final condition is depicted by

$$\boxed{i \neq m \land x \neq a[i,j])}$$

Now let us develop corpus of the program.

8.2   Internals

Let us recall our stated variant:

Invariant :

$$\boxed{0 \leq m \land 0 \leq j < n \land} \land$$

$$\boxed{\text{searcheable-region is bounded by } (m - i) * n - j}$$

Let us try to understand what is meant by the last part of this variant which stands for *searcheable-region is bounded by* $(m - i) * n - j$?

All we were trying to achieve was to contract the search space till the sought after value is found which is nothing but the region depicted by

$$\boxed{(m - i) * n - j}$$

This contraction takes place as long as both the invariant and the condition hold true which implies that

$$\boxed{i < m \land j < n \land x \neq a[i,j]}$$

This will help move the entry a[i, j] from unexplored search space to already explored search space. Easiest way to achieve this is $j \longleftarrow j + 1$, but in order to maintain the invariant it has to satisfy $j < n - 1$.

So we have a beautiful expression as result of this analysis so far :

if $j < n - 1$ then $j \leftarrow j + 1$

In case of $j \geq n - 1$, we can have $j = n - 1$ because the invariant is true.

Let us take the case of a[i, n - 1], which is the rightmost element of ith row. To move this point into the already searched region we can move it to the start of the next row, i.e., $(i \leftarrow i+1$ and $j = 0)^2$. Simple enough.

8.2.1 Putting together

Algorithm 21 Searching in a 2D Array

1: $i \leftarrow 0$
2: $j \leftarrow 0$
3: **function** 2D-SEARCH(a[0..m-1, 0..n-1], x)
4:    **while** $i \neq m$ **and** $x \neq a[i, j]$ **do**
5:       **if** $j < n - 1$ **then**
6:          $j \leftarrow j + 1$
7:       **else if** $j == n - 1$ **then**
8:          $i \leftarrow i + 1$
9:          $j \leftarrow 0$
10:      **end if**
11:    **end while**
12: **end function**

8.2.2 C++11 Implementation

Let us try programming this algorithm in a real language, say C++11 to bring ourselves at workplace-setting environment:

Program 8.1: searching 2D Array

```cpp
#include <algorithm>
#include <array>

using Point = std::pair<int, int>;

template <int m, int n>
using TwoDimArray =
    std::array<std::array<int, n>, m>;

template <int m, int n>
Point search_2darray(TwoDimArray<m, n> & a,
                     int x)
{
    Point p(-1, -1);

    int i = 0, j = 0;

    while((i != m) && (x != a[i][j]))
    {
        if(j < n - 1)
        {
            j += 1;
        }
        else if(j == n - 1)
        {
            i += 1;
            j = 0;
        }
    }

    p.first = i;
    p.second = j;
```

---
[2]it was chosen so to take care when j = n

```
33
34      return p;
35 }
```

Please note that point is initialized with (-1, -1) to mark sentinel conditions which in our case stands for unsuccessful search leading to the value being not found in array.

8.2.3 Usage

Program 8.2: Search for 6 : yields a : 2 2

```
1 #include "2darray_search.hpp"
2 #include <iostream>
3
4 int main()
5 {
6     TwoDimArray<4, 4> a = {
7                             12, 2, 83, 5,
8                             30, 14, 15, 16,
9                             13, 5, 6, 81,
10                            23, 6, 7, 19
11                          };
12
13    Point p = search_2darray<4, 4>(a, 6);
14
15    std::cout << "6 is found at : a["
16             << p.first << "][" << p.second << "]"
17             << std::endl;
18 }
```

This prints:

```
6 is found at : a[2][2]
```

8.2.4 Alternative Program

We can simplify it further to look like as follows:

Algorithm 22 Searching in a 2D Array : Another Program

1: $i \leftarrow 0$
2: $j \leftarrow 0$
3: **function** 2D-SEARCH(a[0..m-1, 0..n-1], x)
4:    **while** $i \neq m$ **and** $x \neq a[i,j]$ **do**
5:        $j \leftarrow j + 1$
6:        **if** $j < n$ **then**
7:            *do nothing*
8:        **else if** $j == n$ **then**
9:            $i \leftarrow i + 1$
10:           $j \leftarrow 0$
11:       **end if**
12:   **end while**
13: **end function**

It could be simplified further to look like

Algorithm 23 Searching in a 2D Array : Another Program(Simplified)

1: $i \leftarrow 0$
2: $j \leftarrow 0$
3: **function** 2D-SEARCH(a[0..m-1, 0..n-1], x)
4: **while** $i \neq m$ **and** $x \neq a[i,j]$ **do**
5: $\quad j \leftarrow j + 1$
6: $\quad$ **if** $j == n$ **then**
7: $\quad\quad i \leftarrow i + 1$
8: $\quad\quad j \leftarrow 0$
9: $\quad$ **end if**
10: **end while**
11: **end function**

Program 8.3: C++11 Version : Searching 2D Array

```cpp
#include <algorithm>
#include <array>

using Point = std::pair<int, int>;

template <int m, int n>
using TwoDimArray =
    std::array<std::array<int, n>, m>;

template <int m, int n>
Point search_2darray(TwoDimArray<m, n> & a,
                     int x)
{
    Point p(-1, -1);

    int i = 0, j = 0;

    while((i != m) && (x != a[i][j]))
    {
        j += 1;
        if(j == n)
        {
            i += 1;
            j = 0;
        }
    }

    p.first = i;
    p.second = j;

    return p;
}
```

Program 8.4: Usage : C++11 Version : Searching 2D Array

```cpp
#include "2darray_search_alt.hpp"
#include <iostream>

int main()
{
    TwoDimArray<4, 4> a = {
                            12, 2, 83, 5,
                            30, 14, 15, 16,
                            13, 5, 6, 81,
                            23, 6, 7, 19
                          };

    Point p = search_2darray<4, 4>(a, 6);
```

```
15    std::cout << "6 is found at : a["
16       << p.first << "]["  << p.second << "]"
17       << std::endl;
18  }
```

8.3   Time Complexity

It is $O(mn)$ because it ends up traversing the entire region $m \times n$ as far as comparison is concerned.

Chapter 9

Select Kth Smallest Element

Problem 9 (*Hoare*)

Design and implement an efficient algorithm to select the Kth Smallest Element of an array.

Solution

9.1 Basic Analysis

9.1.1 Simultaneous Min-Max Algorithm

Before embarking on this selection problem, let us work out a general scheme of finding maximum and minimum of the input sequence. Min-max algorithms are ubiquitous in various applications specially geometric ones. In this section we will revisit several versions with primary focus being finding the most efficient one.

Design an efficient algorithm to find the minimum and maximum of an integer sequence simultaneously.

Let us revisit a typical set-up for finding the maximum of an integer sequence where we end up examine each element of the sequence in turn along with keeping track of the largest element seen so far.

Algorithm 24 Maximum of a sequence

1: **function** MAXVAL(a, l, r)
2:      $0 \leq n$
3:      $a[k] \geq a[0..n-1]$
4:      $i \leftarrow 1$
5:      $k \leftarrow 0$
6:      **while** $0 \leq n$ **do**
7:          **if** $a[i] \leq a[k]$ **then**
8:              *do nothing*
9:          **else if** $a[i] \geq a[k]$ **then**
10:              $k \leftarrow i$
11:          **end if**
12:          $i \leftarrow i + 1$
13:      **end while**
14:      **return** k
15: **end function**

Program 9.1: Finding Maximum in an integer array

```cpp
#include <vector>
#include <algorithm>
#include <cassert>

template <typename T>
size_t maxValArray(std::vector<T> & v)
{
    size_t i = 1, k = 0;
    size_t n = v.size();

    while(i <= n)
    {
        if(v[i] >= v[k]) k = i;
        ++i;
    }

    assert(v[k] == *std::max_element(v.begin(),
                                     v.end())));
    return k;
}

int main()
{
    std::vector<int> v {10, 12, 2, 8, 5, 20, 7};
    maxValArray(v);
}
```

As can be seen that this doesn't address the scenario in presence of multiple occurrences. Let us put forth obvious solutions.

Program 9.2: Finding First Maximum in an integer array

```cpp
template <typename ForwardIterator>
ForwardIterator first_max_element(
    ForwardIter first, ForwardIter last)
{
    if (first == last) return last;
    ForwardIter max_result = first;
    while (++first != last)
    {
        if (*max_result < *first)
            max_result = first;
    }
    return max_result;
}
```

Program 9.3: Finding First Maximum Satisfying Predicate

```cpp
#include <boost/iterator_adaptors.hpp>

template <typename ForwardIterator,
          typename Predicate>
ForwardIterator
first_max_element_if(ForwardIter first,
                     ForwardIter last,
                     Predicate pred)
{
    return first_max_element(
        boost::make_filter_iterator(first, last,
                                    pred),
        boost::make_filter_iterator(last, last,
                                    pred)
    );
}
```

Program 9.4: Finding First Minimum in an integer array

```
1  template <typename ForwardIterator>
2  ForwardIterator first_min_element(
3      ForwardIter first, ForwardIter last)
4  {
5      if (first == last) return last;
6      ForwardIter min_result = first;
7      while (++first != last)
8      {
9          if (*first < *min_result)
10             min_result = first;
11     }
12     return min_result;
13 }
```

Please note that :

Program 9.5: Ordering Equivalence

```
1  std::min_element(v.begin(), v.end(),
2                   std::less<int>())
3  ==
4  std::max_element(v.begin(), v.end(),
5                   std::greater<int>())
```

Program 9.6: Finding Last Maximum in an integer array

```
1  template <typename ForwardIterator>
2  ForwardIterator last_max_element(
3      ForwardIter first, ForwardIter last)
4  {
5      if (first == last) return last;
6      ForwardIter max_result = first;
7      while (++first != last)
8      {
9          if (*first < *max_result)
10             max_result = first;
11     }
12     return max_result;
13 }
```

Program 9.7: Finding Last Minimum in an integer array

```
1  template <typename ForwardIterator>
2  ForwardIterator last_min_element(
3      ForwardIter first, ForwardIter last)
4  {
5      if (first == last) return last;
6      ForwardIter min_result = first;
7      while (++first != last)
8      {
9          if (*min_result < *first)
10             min_result = first;
11     }
12     return min_result;
13 }
```

Please note that:

Program 9.8: Another Ordering Equivalence

```
1  std::reverse_iterator(
```

```
2        first_min_element(v.begin(), v.end(),
3                            std::less<int>())))
4 ==
5 last_max_element(v.rbegin(), v.rend(),
6                    std::greater<int>())
```

All of these algorithms work in similar way requiring $n - 1$ comparisons in worst case.

How about simultaneously finding maximum and minimum of the sequence? Naively, we can get this done in two passes : once for finding maximum and another for finding minimum : total of $2n - 2$ comparisons. But we can definitely do better if we confine ourselves to a single pass and reply on maintaining maximum and minimum elements seen so far. Instead of picking one element and probing it against the current maximum or minimum, we can rather examine two elements at a time treating them as pairs. The process goes like this:

1. Maintain the minimum and maximum of elements seen so far.

2. Don't compare each element to the minimum and maximum separately, which requires two comparisons per element.

3. Pick up the elements in pairs.

4. Compare the elements of a pair to each other.

5. Then compare the larger element to the maximum so far, and compare the smaller element to the minimum so far.

The above requires only three comparisons per two elements. Setting up the initial values for the min and max depends on whether n is odd or even.

- If n is even, compare the first two elements and assign the larger to max and the smaller to min.

  This needs one initial comparison and then $\frac{3(n-2)}{2}$ more comparisons. Thus total number of comparisons $=$

  $1 + \frac{3(n-2)}{2}$

  $= 1 + \frac{3n-6)}{2}$

  $= 1 + \frac{3n}{2} - 3$

  $= \frac{3n}{2} - 2.$

- If n is odd, set both min and max to the first element. Then process the rest of the elements in pairs. This needs a total of $\frac{3(n-1)}{2}$ comparisons.

Program 9.9: C++ Implementation of first min and first max

```
1 template <typename ForwardIterator>
2 std::pair<ForwardIterator, ForwardIterator>
3 first_min_first_max_element(
4     ForwardIterator first,
5     ForwardIterator last)
6 {
7     if (first == last)
8         return std::make_pair(last, last);
9
10    ForwardIterator min_result,
11                    max_result = first;
12
13    // if only one element
14    ForwardIterator second = first; ++second;
15
16    if (second == last)
17    return std::make_pair(min_result,
18                          max_result);
19
20    // treat first pair separately
```

```
21      //(only one comparison for
22      //first two elements)
23      ForwardIterator
24        potential_min_result = last;
25
26      if (*first < *second) max_result = second;
27      else
28      {
29          min_result = second;
30          potential_min_result = first;
31      }
32
33      // then each element by pairs,
34      // with at most 3 comparisons per pair
35      first = ++second;
36
37      if (first != last) ++second;
38
39      while (second != last)
40      {
41          if (*first < *second)
42          {
43              if (*first < *min_result)
44              {
45                  min_result = first;
46                  potential_min_result = last;
47              }
48
49              if (*max_result < *second)
50                  max_result = second;
51          }
52          else
53          {
54              if (*second < *min_result)
55              {
56                  min_result = second;
57                  potential_min_result = first;
58              }
59
60              if (*max_result < *first)
61                  max_result = first;
62          }
63
64          first = ++second;
65
66          if (first != last) ++second;
67      }
68
69      // if odd number of elements,
70      //treat last element
71      if (first != last)
72      { // odd number of elements
73          if (*first < *min_result)
74          {
75              min_result = first;
76              potential_min_result = last;
77          }
78          else if (*max_result < *first)
79              max_result = first;
80      }
81
82      // resolve min_result being incorrect
83      // with one extra comparison
84      // (in which case potential_min_result
85      // is necessarily the
```

```
86      // correct result)
87      if (potential_min_result != last &&
88          !(*min_result < *potential_min_result))
89      min_result = potential_min_result;
90
91      return
92          std::make_pair(min_result, max_result);
93 }
```

Please note that only one comparison is required for first two elements(aka first pair). The above requires at most three comparisons per pair.

In similar spirit, there are multiple combinations possible like:

- first_min_first_max_element
- first_min_last_max_element
- last_min_first_max_element
- last_min_last_max_element

Let us look at the implementation of first_min_last_max_element as inspiration.

Program 9.10: first_min_last_max_element

```
 1 template <typename ForwardIterator>
 2 std::pair<ForwardIterator, ForwardIterator>
 3 first_min_last_max_element(
 4     ForwardIterator first,
 5     ForwardIterator last)
 6 {
 7     if (first == last)
 8         return std::make_pair(last, last);
 9
10     ForwardIterator min_result,
11                     max_result = first;
12
13     ForwardIterator second = ++first;
14
15     if (second == last)
16     return std::make_pair(min_result,
17                           max_result);
18
19     if (*second < *min_result)
20         min_result = second;
21     else max_result = second;
22
23     first = ++second;
24
25     if (first != last) ++second;
26
27     while (second != last)
28     {
29         if (!(*second < *first))
30         {
31             if (*first < *min_result)
32                 min_result = first;
33             if (!(*second < *max_result))
34                 max_result = second;
35         }
36         else
37         {
38             if (*second < *min_result)
39                 min_result = second;
40             if (!(*first < *max_result))
41                 max_result = first;
42         }
43
```

```
44          first = ++second;
45
46          if (first != last) ++second;
47      }
48
49      if (first != last)
50      {
51          if (*first < *min_result)
52              min_result = first;
53          else if (!(*first < *max_result))
54              max_result = first;
55      }
56      return std::make_pair(min_result, max_result);
57 }
```

9.1.2 Generic Select

Selection can be reduced to sorting by sorting the sequence and then extracting the sought after element. This method is more efficient when many selections need to be made from a sequence, in which case only one initial, so-called expensive sort is needed, followed by many relatively less expensive extraction operations, usually in amortized constant time. In general, this method requires $O(n \log n)$ time, where n is the length of the sequence.

Let us try using similar ideas as in finding minimum and maximum of a given sequence for finding the kth smallest or k^{th} largest element in a sequence.

Algorithm 25 Generic Kth Select Minimum

1: **function** GENERIC-KTH-MIN-SELECT(a, l, r, k)
2:     $numElements \leftarrow r - l + 1$
3:     **for** $i \leftarrow 1, k$ **do**
4:         $minIndex \leftarrow i$
5:         $minVal \leftarrow a[i]$
6:         **for** $j \leftarrow i + 1, numElements$ **do**
7:             **if** $a[j] < minVal$ **then**
8:                 $minIndex \leftarrow j$
9:                 $minVal \leftarrow a[j]$
10:             **end if**
11:         **end for**
12:         $swap(a[i], a[minIndex])$
13:     **end for**
14:     **return** $a[k]$
15: **end function**

Program 9.11: Generic Kth Select Minimum

```
1 #include <algorithm>
2 #include <utility>
3 #include <vector>
4 #include <cassert>
5
6 int generic_kth_minselect(std::vector<int> & a,
7                           size_t k)
8 {
9      size_t minIndex = 0;
10     size_t minVal = a[0];
11
12     size_t numElements = a.size();
```

```
13
14    for ( size_t  i  =  0;   i  <  k;   ++i )
15    {
16        minIndex = i ;
17        minVal = a[ i ];
18
19        for ( size_t  j  =  i  +  1;
20                 j  <  numElements;   ++j )
21        {
22            minIndex = j ;
23            minVal = a[ j ];
24        }
25        std :: swap( a[ i ],  a[ minIndex ]) ;
26    }
27    return a[k − 1];
28 }
29
30
31 int  main ()
32 {
33    std :: vector<int>  v  {1,  23,  12,  9,  30,  2,  50};
34
35    int  fourth_min  =  generic_kth_minselect( v,  4 );
36
37    assert( fourth_min  ==  12 );
38 }
```

As can be seen that time complexity of this inefficient selection algorithm is $O(kn)$, where n is the length of the sequence, which is acceptable when k is small enough. It works by simply finding the most minimum element and moving it to the beginning until we reach our desired index, i.e., k. It resembles a *partial selection sort*.

9.2   Randomized Quick Select Algorithm

Let us recall RANDOMIZED-PARTITION and RANDOMIZED-QUICKSORT algorithms to help us build an efficient selection algorithm.

Algorithm 26 Partitioning a sequence

1: **function** PARTITION(a, l, r)
2:     $p \leftarrow a[r]$
3:     $i \leftarrow l - 1$
4:     **for** $j \leftarrow l,\ r - 1$ **do**
5:         **if** $a[j] \leq p$ **then**
6:             $i \leftarrow i + 1$
7:             $swap(a[i], a[j])$
8:         **end if**
9:     **end for**
10:     **return** $i + 1$
11: **end function**

Algorithm 27 Randomized Partition Algorithm

1: **function** RANDOMIZED-PARTITION(a, l, r)
2:     $i \leftarrow random(l, r)$
3:     $swap(a[r], a[i])$
4:     **return** PARTITION(a, l, r)
5: **end function**

Algorithm 28 Randomized Quicksort Algorithm

1: **function** RANDOMIZED-QUICKSORT(a, l, r)
2:     $p \leftarrow$ RANDOMIZED-PARTITION(a, l, r)
3:     RANDOMIZED-QUICKSORT$(a, l, p - 1)$
4:     RANDOMIZED-QUICKSORT$(a, p + 1, r)$
5: **end function**

Let us model the algorithm *randomized-select* based on *randomized-quicksort*, but unlike quicksort, which involves partitioning the input array followed by processing both sides of the partition recursively, *randomized-select* works on only one side of the partition, thus throwing away the other partition.

9.2.1 Algorithm

Algorithm 29 Randomized Kth Min Select Algorithm

1: **function** RANDOMIZED-KTH-MIN-SELECT(a, l, r, k)
2:     $p \leftarrow$ RANDOMIZED-PARTITION(a, l, r)
3:     $pdist \leftarrow p - l + 1$
4:     **if** k == mid **then**
5:         **return** $a[p]$
6:     **else if** k < pdist **then**
7:         **return** RANDOMIZED-KTH-MIN-SELECT$(a, l, p - 1, k)$
8:     **else if** k > pdist **then**
9:         **return** RANDOMIZED-KTH-MIN-SELECT$(a, p + 1, r, k - pdist)$
10:     **end if**
11: **end function**

And it is not that difficult to see that average case time complexity of the algorithm RANDOMIZED-KTH-MIN-SELECT is $\Theta(n)$ and worst case time complexity is $\Theta(n^2)$, assuming that the elements are distinct.

9.2.2 C++11 Implementation

Program 9.12: Randomized version of Kth Select Minimum

```
1 #include <utility>
2 #include <cassert>
3 #include <cstdlib>
4
5 int partition(int a[], int l, int r)
6 {
7     int p = a[r];
8     int i = l - 1;
9
10     for(int j = l; j <= r - 1; j++)
11     {
12         if(a[j] <= p)
13         {
14             i = i + 1;
15             std::swap(a[i], a[j]);
16         }
17     }
18
19     std::swap(a[i + 1], a[r]);
```

```
20
21      return i + 1;
22 }
23
24
25 int randomized_partition(int a[], int l, int r)
26 {
27      int i = l + std::rand() % (r - l + 1);
28      std::swap(a[r], a[i]);
29      return partition(a, l, r);
30 }
31
32
33 int randomized_select(int a[], int l, int r,
34                       size_t k)
35 {
36      int p, pdist;
37      if(l < r)
38      {
39          p = randomized_partition(a, l, r);
40
41          pdist = p - l + 1;
42
43          if(k == pdist) // pivot is the element
44              return a[p];
45          else if(k < pdist)
46              return randomized_select(
47                      a, l, p - 1, k);
48          else // k > pdist
49              return randomized_select(
50                      a, p + 1, r, k - pdist);
51      }
52 }
53
54
55 int main()
56 {
57      int a[] = {8, 1, 6, 4, 0, 3, 9, 5};
58
59      int sixth_min =
60          randomized_select(a, 0, 7, 6);
61
62      assert(sixth_min == 8);
63 }
```

RANDOMIZED-KTH-MIN-SELECT differs from
RANDOMIZED-QUICKSORT because it recurses on one side of the partition only. After
the call to RANDOMIZED-PARTITION, the sequence $a[l..r]$ is partitioned into two subsequences $a[l..p-1]$ and $a[p+1..r]$, along with a pivot element $a[p]$.

- The elements of sub-sequence $a[l..p-1]$ are all $\leq a[p]$.
- The elements of sub-sequence $a[p+1..r]$ are all $> a[p]$.
- The pivot element is the $pdist^{th}$ element of the sub-sequence $a[l..r]$, where $pdist = pl + 1$.
- If the pivot element is the kth smallest element (i.e., k = pdist), return A[p].
- Otherwise, recurse on the sub-sequence containing the kth smallest element.
    - If $k < pdist$, this sub-sequence is $a[l..p-1]$ and we want the kth smallest element.
    - If $k > pdist$, this sub-sequence is $a[p+1..r]$ and, since there are $pdist$ elements in $a[l..r]$ that precede $a[p+1..r]$, we want the $(k-pdist)^{th}$ smallest element of this sub-sequence.

It resembles a *partial quicksort*, generating and partitioning only $O(\log n)$ of its
$O(n)$ partitions. This simple algorithm has expected linear performance, and, like

quicksort, has quite good performance in practice. It is also an *in-place* algorithm, requiring only constant memory overhead, since the tail recursion can be eliminated with an equivalent iterative version as shown in the next section. In a *tail recursion*, the call is always the last action in an algorithm. A tail-recursive algorithm can always be transformed into an equivalent iterative algorithm with a *while* loop as shown ahead.

9.2.3 Iterative Version of Quick Select Algorithm

Algorithm 30 Iterative Version of Quick Select Algorithm

```
 1: function RANDOMIZED-KTH-MIN-SELECT(a, l, r, k)
 2:     while l < r do
 3:         p ← RANDOMIZED-PARTITION(a, l, r)
 4:         pdist ← p − l + 1
 5:         if k == mid then
 6:             return a[p]
 7:         else if k < pdist then
 8:             r ← p − 1
 9:         else if k > pdist then
10:             l ← p + 1
11:             k ← k − pdist
12:         end if
13:     end while
14: end function
```

Now, it is relatively easy to implement this algorithm in your favorite programming language. We leave this as an exercise to the reader.

Chapter 10

Searching in Possibly Empty Two Dimensional Sequence

Problem 10 (*Gries*)

Design a algorithm to search for a given integer x in a 2-dimensional array a[0..m][0..n] where $0 < m$ and $0 < n$. In case of multiple occurrences, it doesn't matter which is found. This is similar to the problem discussed earlier except that here the array may be empty, i.e., it may have 0 rows or 0 columns.

Solution

10.1 Basic Analysis

The algorithm should find the position of a given integer x in the array a, i.e., the algorithm should find i and j such that

- $\boxed{x = a[i,j]}$, or
- $i = m$.

Let us treat the input array as some kind of a rectangular region.

The problem demands that the integer x does exist somewhere in this region. Let us label this condition as *Input Assertion* or *Precondition*.

10.1.1   Precondition (aka *Input Assertion*)

$$\boxed{x \in a[0..m - 1, 0..n - 1]}$$

i.e., x is present somewhere in this rectangular region a.

After the program terminates successfully, x has to be found in a rectangular region of a where the rectangular region consists of just one row and column. Let us label this condition as *Output Assertion* or *Result Assertion* or *Postcondition*.

10.1.2   Postcondition (aka *Result Assertion*)

After the program terminates successfully, then x is in a rectangular region of a where the rectangular region consists of just one row and column, i.e., x is present at i^{th} row and j^{th} column of a, or if this is not possible then i = m, i.e., if x is not found in the array, i.e., if $x \neq a[i, j]$, then i = m.

$$\boxed{(0 \leq i \leq m - 1 \wedge 0 \leq j \leq n - 1}$$

$$\boxed{\wedge x = a[i, j]) \vee (i = m \wedge x \notin a)}$$

10.1.3   Invariant

The invariant states that x is not in the already-searched rows a[0..i - 1] and not in the already-searched columns a[i, 0..j - 1] of the current row i.

Invariant :

$$\boxed{0 \leq m \wedge 0 \leq j \leq n} \wedge$$

$\boxed{\text{searcheable-region is bounded by } (m - i) * n - j + m - i}$, i.e., the bound function is the sum of number of values in the untested section and the number of rows in the untested section represented by $(m - i) * n - j + m - i$. The extra value $m - i$ is required here because j can take up the boundary value n, i.e., $j = n$. As an astute reader, you must have noticed that now the variant includes $j \leq n$, instead of $j < n$. This is required here because the number of columns, n, could be 0 here.

Initialization step is same as discussed earlier.

10.1.4   Condition

Similar to the problem discussed earlier, we can think about $j \leftarrow j + 1$ and/or $i \leftarrow i + 1$ to maintain the invariance.

$$\boxed{\text{if } i \neq m \wedge (j \geq n \text{ and } x \neq a[i,j]) \text{ then } j \leftarrow j + 1}$$

Taking this as a condition, the program can terminate when $i < m \wedge j == n$. If x is not found in the very first row, then this will terminate. So we need to some suitable condition for handling increase of i as well. We can try $i \leftarrow i+1$ but this is only possible till $i < m$ and it can maintain the invariant only if the $x \notin a[i, 0..n]$, so we can think of additional condition being $j == n \implies j = 0$ to maintain the condition on the ith row.

Algorithm 31 Searching in a possibly empty 2D Array

```
1:  i ← 0
2:  j ← 0
3:  function 2D-SEARCH(a[0..m-1, 0..n-1], x)
4:      while i ≠ m and j ≠ n and x ≠ a[i, j] do
5:          j ← j + 1
6:          if i ≠ m and j == n then
7:              i ← i + 1
8:              j ← 0
9:          end if
10:     end while
11: end function
```

10.1.5   C++11 Implementation

Program 10.1: Searching 2D Array
```
1 #include <algorithm>
```

```
 2#include <array>
 3
 4 using Point = std::pair<int, int>;
 5
 6 template <int m, int n>
 7 using TwoDimArray =
 8    std::array<std::array<int, n>, m>;
 9
10 template <int m, int n>
11 Point search_2darray(TwoDimArray<m, n> & a,
12                       int x)
13 {
14     Point p(-1, -1);
15
16     int i = 0, j = 0;
17
18     while((i != m) && (j != n) && (x != a[i][j]))
19     {
20         j += 1;
21         if((i != m) && (j == n))
22         {
23             i += 1;
24             j = 0;
25         }
26     }
27
28     p.first = i;
29     p.second = j;
30
31     return p;
32 }
```

10.1.6   Usage

Program 10.2: Search for 6 : yields a 2 2

```
 1#include "2darray_search_contd.hpp"
 2#include <iostream>
 3
 4 int main()
 5 {
 6     TwoDimArray<4, 4> a = {
 7                            12, 2, 83, 5,
 8                            30, 14, 15, 16,
 9                            13, 5, 6, 81,
10                            23, 6, 7, 19
11                          };
12
13     Point p = search_2darray<4, 4>(a, 6);
14
15     std::cout << "6 is found at : a["
16        << p.first << "][" << p.second << "]"
17        << std::endl;
18
19 }
```

10.2   Time Complexity

It is $O(mn)$ because it ends up traversing the entire region $m \times n$ as far as comparison is concerned.

10.3   Correctness

As discussed in the problem discussed earlier, let us try proving correctness of the program developed by proving the veracity of *Postcondition* upon termination, i.e.,

$$\boxed{Invariant \wedge Condition - Complement \implies Postcondition}$$

Please note that the algorithm has 2 conditions namely

1. $i \neq m \wedge j \neq n$. If this is false $\implies i == m$ may be true. In this case, the invariant implies that $x \notin a$, i.e., x is not present in a[0..m - 1, j].

2. $i \neq m \wedge j == n$. (If this is false and $i \neq m$) $\implies j \neq n$.

Therefore the first condition being false $\implies x = a[i, j]$.

Hence if both conditions stated above are false then the following condition holds true:

$$\boxed{(i == m) \vee (i \neq m \wedge j \neq n \wedge x == a[i, j])}$$

Complement of this condition in conjunction with invariant $\implies$ the result assertion, which proves correctness of our program developed above.

Chapter 11

The Celebrity Problem

Problem 11

Among n persons, a celebrity is defined as someone who is known by everyone but does not know anyone. The problem is to identity the celebrity, if one exists, by asking questions only of the form, "Excuse me, do you know the person over there?" The assumption is that all the answers are correct, and that even the celebrity will answer. The goal is to minimize the number of questions.

Solution

Since there are $\frac{n(n-1)}{2}$ pairs of persons, there us potentially a need to ask *n(n - 1)* questions, in the worst case, if the questions are asked arbitrarily. It is not clear that we can do better in the worst case.

11.1 Graph based approach

We can use a graph-theoretical formulation. We can build a directed graph $G = (V, E)$ (represented by, say, its incident matrix) with the vertices corresponding to the persons and an edge from u to v if person u knows person v. We define a *sink* of a directed graph to be a vertex with indegree $n - 1$ and outdegree 0.

> *A celebrity corresponds to a sink of the graph.*

We note that a graph can have at most one sink. The input to the problem corresponds to an $n \times n$ adjacency matrix, whose ij entry is 1 if the ith person knows the jth peson, and 0 otherwise.

With this formulation, the problem can be reworded as:

> *Given an $n \times n$ adjacency matrix, determine whether $\exists$ an i | all the entries in the ith column (except for the $(ii)^{th}$ entry) are 1, and all the entries in the ith row (except for the $(ii)^{th}$ entry) are 0.*

11.1.1 Inductive approach

The base case of two persons is simple. Let us consider the difference between the problem with $n - 1$ persons and that with n persons. We assume that we can find the celebrity among the first $n - 1$ persons by induction. Since there is at most one celebrity, there are three possibilities :

1. the celebrity is among the first $n - 1$
2. the celebrity is the nth person, or

3. there is no celebrity.

The first case is the easiest to handle. We need only to check that the nth person knows the celebrity, and that the celebrity does not know the nth person. The other two cases are more difficult because, to determine whether the nth person is the celebrity, we may need to ask $2(n-1)$ questions. If we ask $2(n-1)$ questions in the nth step, then the total number of questions will be $n(n-1)$, which is what we are trying to avoid so far ! We definitely need another approach.

The trick here is to consider the problem *backward*. It may be hard to identify a celebrity, but it is probably easier to identify someone as a *non-celebrity*. After all, there are definitely more non-celebrities than celebrities. If we eliminate someone from consideration, then we reduce the size of the problem from n to $n-1$. Moreover, we do not need to eliminate someone specific; anyone will do. Suppose that we ask Alice whether she knows Bob. If she does, then she cannot be a celebrity; if she does not, then Bob cannot be a celebrity. We can eliminate one of them with one question.

We now consider again the three cases with which we started. We do not just take an arbitrary person as the nth person. We use the idea in the last paragraph to eliminate either Alice or Bob, then solve the problem for the other $n-1$ persons. We are guaranteed that *case 2* will not occur, since the person eliminated cannot be the celebrity. Furthermore, if *case 3* occurs, namely, there is no celebrity among the $n-1$ persons, then there is no celebrity among the n persons. Only *case 1* remains, but this case is easy. If there is a celebrity among the $n-1$ persons, it takes two more questions to verify that this is a celebrity for the whole set. Otherwise there is no celebrity.

11.2   Optimal Algorithm

The algorithm proceeds as follows. We ask u whether she knows v, and eliminate either u or v according to the answer. Let us assume that we eliminate u. We then find (by induction) a celebrity among the remaining $n-1$ persons. If there is no celebrity, the algorithm terminates; otherwise we check that u knows the celebrity and that the celebrity does not know u.

11.2.1   Implementation

It is more efficient to implement the celebrity algorithm iteratively, rather than recursively. The algorithm is divided into *two* phases:

1. *elimination phase* : In the first phase, we eliminate all but one candidate.

2. *verification phase* : In the second phase, we check whether this candidate is indeed the celebrity.

We start with n candidates and for the sake of this discussion, let us assume that they are stored in a stack. For each pair of candidates, we can eliminate one candidate by asking one question : *whether one of them knows the other*. We start by taking the first two candidates from the stack, and eliminating one of them. Then, is each step, we have one remaining candidate, and, as long as the stack is nonempty, we take one additional candidate from the stack, and eliminate one of these two candidates. When the stack becomes empty, one candidate remains. We then check that this candidate is indeed the celebrity.

Algorithm 32 Celebrity Algorithm

1: **Input** : an $n \times n$ boolean matrix **M**.
2: **Output** : a celebrity, or *no celebrity* if there is no celebrity.
3: **function** CELEBRITY(M)
4:   $i \leftarrow 1$
5:   $j \leftarrow 2$
6:   $next \leftarrow 3$ ▷ In the first phase we eliminate all but one candidate
7:   **while** $next \leq n + 1$ **do**
8:      **if** M[i, j] **then**
9:         $i \leftarrow next$
10:     **else**
11:        $j \leftarrow next$
12:     **end if**
13:     $next \leftarrow next + 1$
14:   **end while**
                                    ▷ One of either i or j is eliminated
15:   **if** $i \leftarrow n + 1$ **then**
16:     $candidate \leftarrow j$
17:   **else**
18:     $candidate \leftarrow i$
19:   **end if**
                                  ▷ Now we check that the candidate is indeed the celebrity
20:   $wrong \leftarrow false$
21:   $k \leftarrow 1$
22:   $M[candidate, candidate] \leftarrow false$ ▷ A dummy variable to pass the test
23:   **while** not wrong **and** $k \leq n$ **do**
24:     **if** $M[candidate, k$ **then**
25:        $wrong \leftarrow true$
26:     **end if**
27:     **if** not $M[k, candidate]$ **then**
28:        **if** $candidate \neq k$ **then**
29:           $wrong \leftarrow true$
30:        **end if**
31:     **end if**
32:     $k \leftarrow k + 1$
33:     **if** not wrong **then**
34:        $celebrity \leftarrow candidate$
35:     **else**
36:        $celebrity \leftarrow 0$ ▷ no celebrity
37:     **end if**
38:   **end while**
39: **end function**

11.2.2 Complexity

At most $3(n - 1)$ questions will be asked :

1. $n - 1$ questions in the first phase to eliminate $n - 1$ persons, and then

2. at most $2(n - 1)$ questions to verify that the candidate is indeed a celebrity.

Notice that the size of the input is not n, but rather $n(n-1)$, which is the number of entries of the matrix. This solution shows that it is possible to identify a celebrity by looking at only $O(n)$ entries in the adjacency matrix, even though a priori the solution may be sensitive to each of the $n(n - 1)$ entries.

11.2.3 Remarks

The key idea in this elegant solution is to reduce the size of the problem from n to $n - 1$ in a clever way. Do not start by simply considering an *arbitrary* input of size $n - 1$ and attempting to extend it. Select a *particular* input of size $n - 1$.

11.3 Uniqueness of Celebrity

In a set S of n people, there can be only one celebrity.

Assume for contradiction that there are two celebrities C_1 and C_2. By definition of celebrity, everyone knows a celebrity. Therefore $\forall \alpha \in S - \{C_1\}$, α knows C_1. Because $C_2 \in S - \{C_1\}$, C_2 knows C_1. But celebrities don't know anyone. Therefore, C_2 is not a celebrity. This contradicts our assumption that C_2 was a celebrity. Therefore the assumption is false. Therefore, we cannot have two celebrities.

The first algorithm is based on a brute-force approach. We essentially look at each pair of people to see if they know each other. If we find a person that knows nobody but is known by all the others, that person is a celebrity:

Algorithm 33 Celebrity Algorithm Brute Force

1: **Input** : set S of n people
2: **Output** : a celebrity, or *no celebrity* if there is no celebrity.
3: **for all** $A \in S$ **do**
4:     **for all** $B \in S - \{A\}$ **do**
5:         **if** A knows B **then**
6:             *Break out of inner loop*
7:         **else**
8:             $C \leftarrow A$
9:         **end if**
10:     **end for**
11: **end for**
12: **for all** $\alpha \in S$ **do**
13:     **if** α does not know C **then**
14:         **return** "No Celebrity"
15:     **end if**
16:     **return** C
17: **end for**

This algorithm runs in $O(n_2)$ time. Can we do better? Yes, we can. The following algorithm is based on the observation that by asking a single question, we can eliminate a person as a possible celebrity. So, if I ask "Does A know B?" and the answer is "no", then B cannot be a celebrity, because a celebrity must be known by everybody else. On the other hand, if the answer is "yes", then A cannot be a celebrity because a celebrity knows nobody. Therefore, with a single question "Does A know B?", we learn something no matter what the answer to the question is. This leads to this algorithm:

Algorithm 34 Celebrity Algorithm Optimized

1: **Input** : set S of n people
2: **Output** : a celebrity, or *no celebrity* if there is no celebrity.
3: $Candidates \leftarrow S$
4: **while** $|Candidates| > 0$ **do**
5:     Choose A and B $|$ $A \in Candidates$ **and** $B \in Candidates$
6:     **if** A knows B **then**
7:         $Candidates \leftarrow Candidates - \{A\}$
8:     **else**
9:         $Candidates \leftarrow Candidates - \{B\}$
10:     **end if**
11: **end while**
12: Let C be the only remaining element of $Candidates$
13: **for all** $\alpha \in S - \{C\}$ **do**
14:     **if** α does not know C **or** C knows α **then**
15:         **return** "No Celebrity"
16:     **end if**
17:     **return** C
18: **end for**

The first loop here runs $n - 1$ times because every time around the loop we eliminate a possibility (and we stop when there is one possibility left). The second loop runs for $n - 1$ times also because we let α take on $|S| - 1$ different values. Therefore the overall running time is in O(n).

The elimination phase maintains a list of possible celebrities. Initially it contains all n people. In each iteration, we delete one person from the list. We exploit the following key observation: *if person 1 knows person 2, then person 1 is not a celebrity; if person 1 does not know person 2, then person 2 is not a celebrity.* Thus, by asking person 1 if he knows person 2, we can eliminate either person 1 or person 2 from the list of possible celebrities. We can use this idea repeatedly to eliminate all people but one, say person. We now verify by brute force whether is a celebrity: for every other person i, we ask person whether he knows person i, and we ask persons i whether they know person. If person always answers no, and the other people always answer yes, the we declare person as the celebrity. Otherwise, we conclude there is no celebrity in this group.

11.4 Correctness

During the elimination phase, we maintain the invariant that is there exists a celebrity, then the celebrity is on the list. We can prove this by induction on the number of iterations. Thus, when elimination phase ends, either person is a celebrity or there is no celebrity. The elimination phase requires exactly $n - 1$ questions, since each question reduces the size on the list by 1. In the verification phase, we ask $n - 1$ questions, and we ask the other $n - 1$ people one question. This phase requires at most $2(n - 1)$ questions, possibly fewer is is not a celebrity. So the total number of questions is $3(n - 1)$. To efficiently implement the elimination phase, we maintain a queue that contains the remaining celebrities. Initially, we insert all n people to the queue. At each iteration we remove the top two elements off the queue, say v and w, and ask v whether he (or she) knows w. Depending on the outcome, we either insert v or w at the end of the queue. Each queue operation rakes $\theta(1)$ time, so the whole process takes $\theta(n)$ time.

11.5 An even better solution

We note that it is possible to save an additional $\log^2 n$ questions in the verification phase by not repeating any questions we already asked during the elimination phase. By maintaining the elements in a queue, the celebrity is involved (i.e., either asked or asked about) at least $\log^2 n$ questions during the elimination phase. This explains why we chose a queue instead of a stack. Also, it is not hard to see that any algorithm must ask at least $2(n-1)$ questions if there exists a celebrity, since we must verify that the celebrity does not know anyone, and that everyone knows the celebrity.

11.6 C++11 Implementation

Program 11.1: Finding Celebrity Program

```cpp
1 #include <iostream>
2 #include <stack>
3 #include <array>
4
5 template <int m, int n>
6 using CelebrityMatrix =
7     std::array<std::array<bool, n>, m>;
8
9 // Person with 2 is the celebrity
10 CelebrityMatrix <4, 4> KnowCeleb =
11     {
12         0, 0, 1, 0,
13         0, 0, 1, 0,
14         0, 0, 0, 0,
15         0, 0, 1, 0
16     };
17
18 template<int Size>
19 int FindCelebrity()
20 {
21     // Handle trivial case of size = 2
22     std::stack<int> person_stack;
23
24     int i;
25     int C; // Celebrity
26
27     i = 0;
28     while(i < Size)
29     {
30         person_stack.push(i);
31         i = i + 1;
32     }
33
34     int A = person_stack.top();
35     person_stack.pop();
36
37     int B = person_stack.top();
38     person_stack.pop();
39
40     while(person_stack.size() != 1)
41     {
42         if( KnowCeleb[A][B] )
43         {
44             A = person_stack.top();
45             person_stack.pop();
46         }
47         else
48         {
49             B = person_stack.top();
```

```
50          person_stack.pop();
51      }
52  }
53
54      // Potential celebrity candidate
55      C = person_stack.top();
56      person_stack.pop();
57
58      // Last candidate was not examined,
59      // it leads one excess comparison (optimize)
60      if(KnowCeleb[C][B])
61          C = B;
62
63      if(KnowCeleb[C][A])
64          C = A;
65
66      i = 0;
67      while(i < Size)
68      {
69          if(C != i)
70          person_stack.push(i);
71          i = i + 1;
72      }
73
74      while(!person_stack.empty())
75      {
76          i = person_stack.top();
77          person_stack.pop();
78
79          // C must not know i
80          if(KnowCeleb[C][i])
81              return −1;
82
83          // i must know C
84          if(!KnowCeleb[i][C])
85              return −1;
86      }
87
88      return C;
89  }
90
91  int main()
92  {
93      int id = FindCelebrity<4>();
94
95      id == −1 ? std::cout << "No celebrity" : std::cout << "
            Celebrity ID " << id;
96  }
```

Chapter 12

Switch and Bulb Problem

Problem 12

Imagine two rooms with no visibility between them. In one room there n numbered light switches $s_1, s_2, \ldots, s_n$. In the other room there are n numbered light bulbs $l_1, l_2, \ldots, l_n$. It is known that each switch turns on and off to exactly one bulb but we do not know anything about the wiring between the switches and the bulbs. Initially we are in the room with the switches. Our job is to tell the exact wiring, i.e. which switch operates which bulb. We are allowed to press any switches and then go to the room with the bulbs and perform an observation. We are not allowed to touch the bulbs : our only source of information is the observation of the bulbs.

The switches are such that their physical appearance does not change when toggled so we have no way of knowing beforehand whether pressing a certain switch leads to turning on or turning off of a bulb. Every switch has, of course, two states only, as any normal light switch.

Describe an algorithm that discovers the wiring with minimum number of observations, i.e. with minimum visits to the room with the bulbs. The algorithm should work iteratively, at each iteration simulating toggling some switches and then simulating an observation by calling some function OBSERVE. *The toggling is simulated by writing into a 0-1 array P[1, . . . , n]. Say, P[i] = 1 means s_i is toggled, and P[i] = 0 means s_i is not toggled. The result of the observation is written in some 0-1 array L[1, . . . , n]. Say, L[i] = 1 means l_i is on, and L[i] = 0 means l_i is off. After every call to* OBSERVE, *the algorithm temporarily halts, the execution is supposed to be transferred to an outside agent and the algorithm resumes after the outside agent finishes writing into L.*

Prove an asymptotic lower bound for the number of observations. Is your algorithm optimal in the asymptotic sense?

Solution

12.1 Algorithm

Our algorithm maintains the following data structures:

- a 0-1 array A[1, . . . , n] to keep the result of the previous observation,
- an array S[1, . . . , n] that refers to the switches. Every element of S is a pointer. Namely, S[i] points to a (doubly) linked list that represents the set of the bulbs, each of which can possibly be connected to s_i according to

currently available information. We call this set of bulbs, *the candidate set* for s_i .

- an array B of positive integers of size 2n. During iteration i, B contains 2i elements that determine a partitioning of S into subarrays. B[2j] and B[2j + 1] are numbers such that B[2j] B[2j + 1] and the pair B[2j], B[2j + 1] represents the subarray S[B[2j], . . . , B[2j + 1]].

- a multitide of doubly linked lists with n elements altogether. They represent a partition of the set of the bulbs. Each element contains an integer that corresponds to the ID of precisely one bulb, and each list represents precisely one candidate set. Initially, there is only one list in this multitude, call this list C. That reflects the fact that at the beginning we have no restrictions on the possible connections between bulbs and switches. At the end, there are n non-empty lists in this multitude. That reflects the fact that at the end we know precisely the wiring between the switches and the bulbs.

12.2 Implementation

Here is the pseudocode. Initially P[ ] is arbitrary.

Algorithm 35 Switches And Bulbs Problem

1: **function** SWITCHES-AND-BULBS
2:     create doubly linked list C of n elements, one for each bulb
3:     create S and set every pointer in it to C
4:     $B \leftarrow [1, n]$
5:     OBSERVE()
6:     copy L into A
7:     **while** there are less than 2n entities in B **do**
8:         **for all** $pair B[2j], B[2j + 1]$ **do** such that B[2j] < B[2j + 1]
9:         $mid \leftarrow \frac{1}{2}(B[2j] + B[2j + 1])$
10:         set $P[B[2j], \ldots, mid]$ to ones
11:         set $P[mid + 1, \ldots, B[2j + 1]]$ to zeros
12:         **end for**
13:         update B so that for each applicable pair B[2j], B[2j + 1] , it is substituted by two pairs <B[2j], mid> and <mid + 1, B[2j + 1]>
14:         OBSERVE()
15:         **for** $i \leftarrow 1$ to n **do**
16:         **if** $A[i] \neq L[i]$ **then**
17:         mark bulb i as changed
18:         **end if**
19:         **for all** list of bulbs **do**
20:         split the list, if necessary, into two lists: changed and unchanged bulbs
21:         **end for**
22:         **for all** element of S **do**
23:         update the pointer to the relevant list of bulbs
24:         **end for**
25:         **end for**
26:     copy L into A
27:     **end while**
28:     **for** $i \leftarrow 1$ to n **do**
29:         **print** the sole element of the list pointed to by S[i]
30:     **end for**
31: **end function**

12.3 Time Complexity Analysis

The query complexity of the algorithm, i.e. the number of calls of OBSERVE, is the number of executions of the while loop plus one. The number of executions of the while loop is logarithmic in n because we split each subarray, delineated by a couple from B, roughly in half, with each execution. So, the number of queries is $\Theta(\log n)$.

Now we prove an $\Omega(\log n)$ lower bound of the number of such queries. We use the decision tree model. The decision tree model is used, for instance, for proving an $\Omega(n \log n)$ lower bound for comparison based sorting. However, the decision trees for comparison based sorting are binary because there are precisely two possible outcomes of each comparison of the kind $a_i < a_j$. In contrast to that, any decision tree that corresponds to the current problem of switches and bulbs has branching factor of 2^n. To why this is true, note that there are precisely 2^n possible outcomes from each observation of the n bulbs.

The current problem is, essentially, computing a permutation, because the mapping from switches to bulbs is a *bijection*. It follows that any decision tree for that problem has to distinguish all possible n! permutations of n elements: if the decision tree has a leaf labeled by at least two permutations then the corresponding algorithm is not correct. It follows that the leaves must be at least n!.

The height of the tree is approximately logarithm to base the branching factor of the number of leaves:

$$\log_{2^n} n! = \frac{\log_2 n!}{\log_2 2^n} = \frac{\Theta(n \log n)}{n} = \Theta(\log n)$$

The height of the tree is a lower bound for the query complexity of any observation-based algorithm for the problem of switches and bulbs. It follows that $\Theta(\log n)$ observations are required if the only testing allowed is direct observation. It follows that algorithm SWITCHES-AND-BULBS is asymptotically optimal with respect to the number of performed observations. ∎

Chapter 13

Interpolation Search

Problem 13

Interpolation search is a method of retrieving a desired record by key in an ordered sequence by using the value of the key and the statistical distribution of the keys. Design and implement the algorithm.

Solution

13.1 Introduction

In binary search, the search space is always cut in half, which guarantees the logarithmic performance. However, if during the search we find a value that is very close to the number we are searching for, say, x, it seems more reasonable to continue the search in that *neighborhood* instead of blindly going to the next half point. In particular, if x is very small, we should start the search somewhere in the beginning of the sequence instead of at the halfway point.

Interpolation search is a method of retrieving a desired record by key in an ordered sequence by using the value of the key and the statistical distribution of the keys.

Consider the way we open a book when we are searching for a certain page number, say 200, and the book consists of 800 pages. Page 200 is thus around the one-fourth mark, and we use this knowledge as an indication of where to open the book. We will probably not hit page 200 on the first try; suppose that we get page 250 instead. We now cut the search to a range of 250 pages, and the desired page is at about the 80 percent mark between page 1 and 250. We now try to go back about $(\frac{1}{5})^{th}$ of the way. We can continue this process until we get close enough to page 200, that we can flip one page at a time. This is exactly the idea behind interpolation search. Instead of cutting the search space by a fixed half, we cut it by an amount that seems the most likely to succeed. This amount is determined by interpolation.

Given a file of 1000 records with keys $X_1 < X_2 < \ldots < X_{1000}$ uniformly distributed between 0 and 1, our task is to find an index $i \mid X_i = 0.7$. It is reasonable to expect that about $0.7 \times 1000 = 700$ keys are lesaa than or equal to 0.7 and the required record should be near the 700th record.

However, looking into the file may reveal that $X_{700} = 0.68 < 0.7$. Although we have not retrieved the record, we can deduce that the desired index lies between 700 and 1000. The corresponding keys are uniformly distributed between 0.68 and

1. The new file contains 300 records. $P_2 = \frac{(0.7-0.68)}{(1-0.68)} = 0.0675$ is the probability that these records have smaller or equal keys; therefore we should now look at the $300 \times 0.675 \approx 20^{th}$ record of the new file.

This process is continued by using the same method; at each iteration either the record is found or the length of the files is decreased.

Interpolation search was first suggested by Peterson as a method for searching in sorted sequences stored in contiguous storage locations.

13.2 Algorithm

Algorithm 36 Interpolation Search Algorithm

1: **Input** : A (a sorted array) and x (the search key).
2: **Output** : *position* (an index $i \mid A[i] = x$, or 0 if no such index exist).
3: **function** INTERPOLATION-SEARCH($A[0..n - 1]$, x)
4:     **if** $x < A[0]$ **or** $x > A[n-1]$ **then**
5:         *position* $\leftarrow 0$ ▷ unsuccessful search
6:     **else**
7:         *position* = INTERPOLATION-SEARCH-HELPER($x, 0, n-1$)
8:     **end if**
9:     **return** *position*
10: **end function**
11: **function** INTERPOLATION-SEARCH-HELPER(x, l, r)
12:     *found* $\leftarrow 0$
13:     **if** $A[l] == x$ **then**
14:         *found* = l
15:     **else if** $l == r$ **or** $A[l] == A[r]$ **then**
16:         *found* = 0
17:     **else**
18:         $next = \left[l + \frac{(x-A[l])(r-l)}{A[r]-A[l]} \right]$
19:         **if** x < A[next] **then**
20:             *found* = INTERPOLATION-SEARCH-HELPER($x, l, next - 1$)
21:         **else**
22:             *found* = INTERPOLATION-SEARCH-HELPER($x, next, r$)
23:         **end if**
24:     **end if**
25:     **return** *found*
26: **end function**

13.3 Complexity

The performance of interpolation search depends not only on the size of the sequence, but also on the input itself. There are inputs for which interpolation search checks every number in the sequence. However, interpolation search is very efficient for inputs consisting of relatively uniformly distributed elements, for example, the pages of a book are uniformly distributed without any doubt. It can be shown that the average number of comparisons performed by interpolation search, where the average is taken over all possible sequences, is $O(\log \log n)$. Although this seems to be an order of magnitude improvement over the performance of binary search, interpolation search is not much better than binary search in practice because

1. unless n is very large, the value of $\log_2 n$ is small enough that the logarithm of it is not much smaller.

2. interpolation search requires more elaborate arithmetic.

13.4   C++ Implementation

Program 13.1: Interpolation Search

```
1 #include <vector>
2 #include <cassert>
3
4 template<typename T>
5 T interpolation_search_helper(T A[], std::size_t l, std::
      size_t r, T value)
6 {
7     std::size_t found = 0, next;
8
9     if(A[l] == value)
10    {
11        found = l;
12    }
13    else if((l == r) || (A[l] == A[r]))
14    {
15        found = 0;
16    }
17    else
18    {
19        next = l + (value - A[l])*(r - l) / (A[r] - A[l]);
20
21        if(value < A[next])
22        {
23            found = interpolation_search_helper(A, l, next
                  - 1, value);
24        }
25        else
26        {
27            found = interpolation_search_helper(A, next, r,
                  value);
28        }
29    }
30
31    return found;
32 }
33
34
35 template<typename T>
36 T interpolation_search(T sorted_array[], std::size_t l, std
      ::size_t r, T value)
37 {
38    std::size_t position = 0;
39
40    if(value < sorted_array[l] || value > sorted_array[r])
41    {
42        position = 0;
43    }
44    else
45    {
46        position = interpolation_search_helper(sorted_array
              , l, r , value);
47    }
48    return position;
49 }
50
51
52 int main()
53 {
```

```
54    int sorted_array[] = {1, 2, 3, 4, 5, 6, 7, 8, 9};
55
56    assert(interpolation_search(sorted_array, 0, 8, 5) ==
         4);
57  }
```

13.5 Remarks

For external search (the file resides on an external device), interpolation search is superior to binary search since the search time is determined by the number of accesses. However, in internal search the computation time of each iteration should also be considered. Computer experiments showed that interpolation search and binary search take approximately the same time. Interpolation search is slightly faster only for files larger than 5000 records. However, using shift operations instead of division in binary search or the use of Fibonaccian search results in faster internal search methods. After a few iterations of interpolation search, we are quite close to the required record. When the difference between the indices of two successive iterations is small, it may be advantageous to switch to sequential search and save computation time.

Chapter 14

The Majority Problem

Problem 14

We are given a set S of n objects $(n \geq 1)$, each of which has a color. Furthermore, we are told that there is a majority color in S, i.e., a color that occurs strictly more than $\frac{n}{2}$ times. We denote this majority color by $mc(S)$. Our task is to find an element of S whose color is equal to $mc(S)$. We are only allowed to use the operation same_color. *This operation takes two arbitrary elements, say x and y, of S, and returns the value*

$$same\_color(x, y) = \begin{cases} true, & \text{if } x \text{ and } y \text{ have the same color.} \\ false, & \text{otherwise.} \end{cases} \qquad (14.1)$$

In particular, we cannot determine the color of any element of S

Solution

14.1 Algorithm

Our algorithm will be based on the following observation.

14.1.1 First Observation

Let x and y be two elements of S that have different colors. Then there is a majority color in the set $S \setminus \{x, y\}$, and

$$mc(S) = mc(S \setminus \{x, y\})$$

14.1.2 Proof

Assume that $mc(S) = red$. Let k be the number of red elements in S. Then we know that $k > \frac{n}{2}$. We have to show that the set $S \setminus \{x, y\}$ contains more than $\frac{(n2)}{2}$ red elements.

14.1.2.1 Case 1

Neither x nor y is red. In this case, the number of red elements in $S \setminus \{x, y\}$ is equal to $k > \frac{n}{2} > \frac{(n2)}{2}$.

14.1.2.2   Case 2

Exactly one x and y is red. In this case, the number of red elements in $S \setminus \{x, y\}$ is equal to $k1 > \frac{n}{2} 1 = \frac{(n2)}{2}$. ∎

14.1.3   Invariant

We maintain the following *invariant*:

1. S is the disjoint union of three sets N, I, and D.
2. All elements of I have the same color.
3. There is a majority color in the set $N \cup I$.
4. $mc(S) = mc(N \cup I)$.

14.1.3.1   Notation

- N ≡ *Not seen yet*
- I ≡ *Identical colors*
- D ≡ *Discarded*

Here is the basic version of our algorithm:

Algorithm 37 Find Majority Simple Algorithm

1: $N \leftarrow S$
2: $I \leftarrow \emptyset$
3: $D \leftarrow \emptyset$
4: **while** $N \neq \emptyset$ **do**
5:    **if** $I == \emptyset$ **then**
6:       *move one element from N to I*
7:    **else**
8:       $x \in N$
9:       $y \in I$
10:      **if** *same_color(x, y)* **then**
11:         *move x from N to I*
12:      **else**
13:         *move y from I to D*
14:         *move x from N to D*
15:      **end if**
16:   **end if**
17: **end while**
18: **return** *an arbitrary element of I*

14.2   A simple representation of the algorithm

Until now, we did not specify how the sets N, I, and D are represented. There turns out to be a very simple way to do this: Let the elements of S be stored in an array $A[1...n]$. We will use two indices i and j to represent the sets N, I, and D:

1. $0 \leq i \leq j - 1 \leq n$
2. $D = A[1..i]$
3. $I = A[i + 1..j - 1]$
4. $N = A[j..n]$

If we *translate* our basic algorithm, then we get the following algorithm:

Algorithm 38 Find Majority Algorithm Revisited

1: $i \leftarrow 0$
2: $j \leftarrow 1$
3: **while** $j \leq n$ **do**
4:   **if** $j \leq i + 1$ **then**
5:     $j \leftarrow j + 1$
6:   **else if** *same_color(A[j], A[i + 1])* **then**
7:     $j \leftarrow j + 1$
8:   **else**
9:     $i \leftarrow i + 1$
10:     $swap(A[j], A[i + 1])$
11:     $i \leftarrow i + 1$
12:     $j \leftarrow j + 1$
13:   **end if**
14: **end while**
15: **return** $A[i + 1]$

If we change the order of the operations, then we get the following algorithm:

Algorithm 39 Find Majority Algorithm Simplified

1: $i \leftarrow 0$
2: $j \leftarrow 1$
3: **while** $j \leq n$ **do**
4:   **if** $j \geq i + 2$ **and** same_color(A[j], A[i + 1]) $==$ *false* **then**
5:     $i \leftarrow i + 2$
6:     $swap(A[j], A[i])$
7:   **end if**
8:   $j \leftarrow j + 1$
9: **end while**
10: **return** $A[i + 1]$

14.2.1 Second Observation

In the pseudocode above, the condition

$$j \geq i + 2 \text{ and } same\_color(A[j], A[i + 1]) == false$$

is equivalent to the condition

$$same\_color(A[j], A[i + 1]) == false$$

14.2.1.1 Proof

Assume that *same_color(A[j], A[i + 1])* = *false*. We have to show that $j \geq i + 2$. We know from the invariant that $j \geq i + 1$. If $j = i + 1$, then same color(A[j], A[i + 1]) = *true*. Therefore, $j \neq i + 1$. It follows that $j \geq i + 2$. ■

Using this observation, we can further simplify the algorithm, and obtain the final algorithm:

Algorithm 40 Find Majority Algorithm Final

```
1: i ← 0
2: j ← 1
3: while j ≤ n do
4:     if same_color(A[j], A[i + 1]) == false then
5:         i ← i + 2
6:         swap(A[j], A[i])
7:     end if
8:     j ← j + 1
9: end while
10: return A[i + 1]
```

Chapter 15

The Plateau Problem

Problem 15

The array $b[0..n-1]$ has n elements, may have duplicate elements, and is sorted. A plateau *of length* p *is a sequence of* p *consecutive elements with the same value. Find the length of the* longest plateau *in b.*

Solution

15.1 Analysis

The value p is the length of the longest plateau if there is a sequence of p equal values and no sequence of $p + 1$ equal values. i.e.

- $b[0..n-1]$ contains a plateau of length p, and
- $b[0..n-1]$ does not contain a plateau of length $p + 1$

Because the array is sorted, a subsection $b[k..j]$ is a *plateau* if and only if its end elements $b[k]$ and $b[j]$ are equal, i.e.

$$0 \le k \le n - p : b[k] = b[k + p - 1]$$
$$\textbf{and}$$
$$0 \le k \le n - p - 1 : b[k] \ne b[k + p]$$

Therefore,

p is the length of the longest plateau of $b[0..i]$ $\iff$ $b[i - p..i]$ is not a plateau

$\implies$ this holds

$$\iff b[i - p] \ne b[i]$$

15.2 Invariant

The length of the *plateau* of an array of length 1 is obviously 1. Using this fact, we can develop an invariant as follows:

$1 \le i \le n$ **and** p is the length of the *longest plateau* of $b[0..i-1]$.

15.3 Algorithm

Now, it is easy to see the full program as follows:

Algorithm 41 The Plateau Problem

1: $i \leftarrow 1$
2: $p \leftarrow 1$
3: **Invariant** : $1 \leq i \leq n$ **and** p is the length of the longest plateau of $b[0..i-1]$
4: **Bound Function** $t = n - i$
5: **function** FIND-PLATEAU($b[0..n-1]$)
6:     **while** $i \neq n$ **do**
7:         **if** $b[i] \neq b[i-p]$ **then**
8:             $i \leftarrow i + 1$
9:         **else if** $b[i] == b[i-p]$ **then**
10:            $i \leftarrow i + 1$
11:            $p \leftarrow p + 1$
12:        **end if**
13:    **end while**
14: **end function**

Please note that this program finds the length of the longest plateau for any array, even if not sorted, as long as all equal values are adjacent.

15.4 Alternative Solution

We can also use the idea that the loop body should investigate one plateau at each iteration. The loop invariant is therefore :

$$0 \leq i \leq n$$
$$\textbf{and}$$
$$p = \text{length of longest plateau of } b[0..i-1]$$
$$\textbf{and}$$
$$i = 0 \textbf{ or } i = n \textbf{ or } b[i-1] \neq b[i]$$

Please note that the length of the longest plateau of an empty array is zero.

Algorithm 42 The Plateau Problem Revisited

```
 1: i ← 1
 2: p ← 1
 3: Invariant :
 4: 0 ≤ i ≤ n
 5: and
 6: p = length of longest plateau of b[0..i − 1]
 7: and
 8: i = 0 or i = n or b[i − 1] ≠ b[i]
 9: Bound Function t = n − i
10: function FIND-PLATEAU(b[0..n-1])
11:     while i ≠ n do
12:         increase i, keeping invariant true
13:         j ← i + 1
14:         Invariant: b[i..j − 1] are all equal; Bound Function: n - j
15:         while j ≠ n and b[j] == b[i] do
16:             j ← j + 1
17:         end while
18:         p ← max(p, j − i)
19:         i ← j
20:     end while
21: end function
```

Chapter 16

Segment Problems

Problem 16

Segment problems involve the computation of a longest or shortest segment that satisfies a certain predicate, usually defined in terms of a given array. Design and implement algorithm to solve such problems.

Solution

16.1 Longest Segments

Let $N \geq 0$ and let $X[0..N)$ be an integer array. We are interested in the length of a longest subsegment $[p..q)$ of $[0..N)$ that satisfies a certain predicate defined in terms of X. Examples of such predicates are :

- all elements are zero : $\forall i : p \leq i < q : X.i = 0$
- the segment is left-minimal : $\forall i : p \leq i < q : X.p \leq X.i$
- the segment contains at most 10 zeros : $(\#i : p \leq i < q : X.i = 0) \leq 10$
- all values are different : $\forall i, j : p \leq i < j < q : X.i \neq X.j$

16.1.1 All Zeros

Let us solve the problem of determining the length of a longest segment of $X[0..N)$ that contains zero only. It is about the simplest longest segment problem one can imagine. This problem can be re-instated as follows:

1: $N : int\{N \geq 0\}$
2: $X : array[0..N)$ of int
3: $r : int$
4: $r = (\mathbf{max}\ p, q : 0 \leq p \leq q \leq N \land (\forall i : p \leq i < q : X.i = 0) : q - p$

Our first step is the introduction of a name for $(\forall i : p \leq i < q : X.i = 0)$. This does not only abbreviate the postcondition, but, more importantly, it enables us to find out which parts of the derivation are independent of the specific form of the predicate.

For $0 \leq p \leq q \leq N$ we define $A.p.q$ by

$$A.p.q \equiv (\forall i : p \leq i < q : X.i = 0)$$

Postcondition R may then be written as

$$R : r = (\textbf{max } p, q : 0 \le p \le q \le N \wedge A.p.q : q - p)$$

What can be said about predicate A? Its term, $X.i = 0$, does not depend on p or q. It holds for empty segments, i.e.,

$$A.n.n \text{ for } 0 \le n \le N$$

Furthermore, A is prefix-closed, i.e., if a segment satisfies A then all prefixes of that segment satisfy A as well. More formally,

$$A.p.q \implies (\forall i : p \le i \le q : A.p.i) \text{ for } 0 \le p \le q \le N$$

and A is postfix-closed:

$$A.p.q \implies (\forall i : p \le i \le q : A.i.q) \text{ for } 0 \le p \le q \le N$$

Since the term, $X.i = 0$, in A neither depends on p nor on q, it does not matter whether we replace in R the constant 0 or the constant N by a variable. We propose as invariants P_0 and P_1 defined by

$$P_0 : r = (\textbf{ max } p, q : 0 \le p \le q \le n \wedge A.p.q : q - p)$$

and

$$P_1 : 0 \le n \le N$$

For the initialization, we derive

$$\textbf{max } p, q : 0 \le p \le q \le 0 \wedge A.p.q. : q - p = \textbf{max } p, q : p = 0 \wedge q = 0 \wedge A.p.q : q - p$$
$$= 0$$

from which we infer that $P_0 \wedge P_1$ is initialized by $n \leftarrow 0$ and $r \leftarrow 0$. For an increase of n by 1 we derive, assuming $P_0 \wedge P_1 \wedge n \ne N$,

$$\textbf{max } p, q : 0 \le p \le q \le n+1 \wedge A.p.q : q - p = \textbf{max }$$
$$p, q : 0 \le p \le q \le n \wedge A.p.q : q - p = \textbf{max (max}$$
$$p : 0 \le p \le n+1 \wedge A.p.(n+1) : n+1-p) = \text{r } \textbf{max (max}$$
$$p : 0 \le p \le n+1 \wedge A.p.(n+1) : n+1-p) = + \text{ distribute over } \textbf{max} \text{ for a}$$
non-empty range, $A.(n+1).(n+1) = \text{r } \textbf{max } (\ n+1+(\textbf{max } p :$
$$0 \le p \le n+1 \wedge A.p(n+1) : -p = \text{r } \textbf{max } (\ n+1-(\textbf{min } p :$$
$$0 \le p \le n+1 \wedge A.p(n+1) : p$$

leading to the introduction of integer variables s and accompanying invariant

$$Q : s = (\textbf{ min } p : 0 \le p \le n \wedge A.p.n : p)$$

From $(\textbf{ min } p : 0 \le p \le 0 \wedge A.p.0 : p) = 0$, we infer that s should be initialized at zero and we obtain a program of the following form:

1: $N \ge 0 \wedge (\forall n : 0 \le n \le N : A.n.n)$
2: $n \leftarrow 0$
3: $r \leftarrow 0$
4: $s \leftarrow 0$
5: **Invariant :** $P_0 \wedge P_1 \wedge Q$
6: *bound* : $N - n$
7: **while** $n \ne N$ **do**
8:     *establish* $Q(n \leftarrow n+1)$
9:     $r \leftarrow \text{r } \textbf{max } (n+1-s)$
10:     $n \leftarrow n+1$
11: **end while** $\triangleright \text{r} = (\textbf{ max } p, q : 0 \le p \le q \le N \wedge A.p.q : q - p)$

16.2   Subproblem

This program leaves "*establish $Q(n \leftarrow n+1)$*" as a subproblem. Since A holds for empty segments, the range of the quantification in Q is non-empty and Q can be written as the conjunction of Q_0, Q_1, and Q_2, defined as

- $Q_0 : 0 \leq s \leq n$
- $Q_1 : A.s.n$
- $Q_2 : (\forall p : 0 \leq p < s : \neg A.p.n$

Since A is prefix-closed, we have $\neg A.p.n \implies \neg A.p.(n+1)$ for $0 \leq p < n$, and, hence

$$Q_2 \implies Q_2(n \leftarrow n+1)$$

We have $Q_0 \implies Q_0(n \leftarrow n+1)$ as well and we conclude

$$Q_0 \wedge Q_2 \wedge A.s.(n+1) \implies Q(n \leftarrow n+1)$$

The fact that $Q_2(n \leftarrow n+1)$ is implied by Q_2 has another consequence. From

$$Q_2(n \leftarrow n+1) \equiv (\forall p : 0 \leq p < s : \neg A.p.(n+1))$$

we infer

$$Q_2 \implies (\ \mathbf{min}\ p : 0 \leq p \leq n+1 \wedge A.p.(n+1) : p) \geq s$$

i.e., only values p for which $s \leq p \leq n+1$ have to be investigated. For $p = n+1$, we know that $A.p.(n+1)$ holds, so we usually start our investigations with the calculation of $A.p.(n+1)$ for $s \leq p \leq n$.

We return to *all zeros*, for which $A.p.q \equiv (\forall i : p \leq i < q : X.i = 0)$, and we compute $A.p.(n+1)$ for $s \leq p \leq n$:

$$A.p.(n+1) \equiv (\forall i : p \leq i < n+1 : X.i = 0) \equiv (\forall i : p \leq i < n : X.n = 0) \wedge X.n = 0 \equiv A.p.n \wedge X.n = 0$$

Hence,

$$Q \wedge X.n = 0 \implies Q(n \leftarrow n+1)$$

and

$$X.n \neq 0 \implies (\forall p : s \leq p \leq n : \neg A.p.(n+1))$$

from which we infer, since $A.(n+1).(n+1)$ holds

$$X.n \neq 0 \implies Q(n \leftarrow n+1)(s \leftarrow n+1)$$

This leads to the following solutions to *all zeros*:

Algorithm 43 All Zeros Program

```
1:  n, s : int
2:  n ← 0
3:  r ← 0
4:  s ← 0
5:  while n ≠ N do
6:      if X.n == 0 then
7:          skip
8:      else if X.n ≠ 0 then
9:          s ← n + 1
10:     end if
11:     r ← r max (n + 1 - s)
12:     n ← n + 1
13: end while
```

Please note that we did not use the postfix-closedness of A.

Chapter 17

Efficient Permutation

Problem 17

Design a program that will generate the n! permutations of the values from 0 through n-1 in such an order that the transition from one permutation to the next is always performed by exactly one swap of two neighbors.

Solution

17.1 Reduction Approach(*to inversion*)

In a permutation each pair of values such that the larger value precedes the smaller one, presents a so-called *inversion*. In particular: the one and only permutation with zero inversions is the one in which the values are placed in monotonically increasing order.

The notion of inversions can be expected to be relevant here because the swapping of two neighbors changes the total number of inversions : i.e. the number of pairs in the wrong order: by (plus or minus) 1, and it is, therefore, suggested to

characterize each permutation by its inversions.

This can be done by introducing n inversion counters inversion[i] for $0 \leq i < n$, where inversion[i] equals the number of inversions between the value i and the values smaller than i.

In other words, inversion[i] equals the number of numbers $< i$, that are placed at *the wrong side* of i, so we can say that

inversion[i] = *the number of inversions between the value i and smaller values.*

From this definition

$$0 \leq inversion[i] \leq i$$

follows;

the total number of inversions of a permutation is the sum of the corresponding inversion[i] values.

i.e., The total number of inversions of the permutation is the sum of all the inversion[i] values.

So it is obvious that:

1. Each permutation defines the inversion[i] values uniquely, and
2. The inverse[i] define the permutation uniquely.

The second point above is easily seen by considering the algorithm constructing the permutation from the inversion[i] values, thus processing these values in the order of increasing i.

So there is a one-to-one correspondence between the n! possible inversion values and the n! permutations. With this insight, the original problem is reduced to the following problem :

which modifications of the inversion value correspond to a swap of neighbors

Each swap of two neighbors changes exactly one inversion[i] value by 1, viz. with i = the larger of the two values swapped. The value of inversion[i] is to be increased if the swap increases the number of inversions; otherwise it is to be decreased.

A feasible sequence of inversion values to be generated is now reasonably obvious: it is the generalization of the Grey-code. For n = 4 it would begin

inversion[0]	inversion[1]	inversion[2]	inversion[3]
0	0	0	0
0	0	0	1
0	0	0	2
0	0	0	3
0	0	1	3
0	0	1	2
0	0	1	1
0	0	1	0
0	0	2	0
0	0	2	1
0	0	2	2
0	0	2	3
0	1	2	3
0	1	2	2
:	:	:	:

17.2   Algorithm

The logic is simple: a number is changeable when

1. it may be increased by 1 $\implies$ if the sum of the numbers to its left is even and it has not reached its maximum value.
2. it may be decreased by 1 $\implies$ if the sum of the numbers to its left is odd and it has not reached its minimum value zero.

Please note that at each step, always the right-most changeable number is changed. It is not difficult to see that in the permutation, the value i is, indeed, swapped with a smaller value.

After having established the value i, such that inversion[i] has to be changed, and, also, whether the value i has to be swapped with its predecessor in the permutation (corresponding to an increase of inversion[i]) or with its successor in the permutation (corresponding to a decrease of inversion[i]), we have to establish the place c in the permutation, where the value i is located, because $\forall j > i$, inversion[j] has an extreme value, c is given by:

$$c = i - inversion[i] + (\text{the number of values } j \mid j > i \, \&\& \, inversion[j] = j)$$

Reason is simple : i is its original position, inversion[i] is the number of smaller elements to the right of it; we have to add to it the number of larger elements in front of the section with *elements* $\leq i$.

17.3 C++ Implementation

Putting this algorithm in C++ code is easy now:

Program 17.1: generate efficient permutation

```cpp
1 #include <iostream>
2 #include <algorithm>
3
4 bool odd(int i)
5 {
6     return i & 1;
7 }
8
9 bool even(int i)
10 {
11     return !odd(i);
12 }
13
14 int main()
15 {
16     const int n = 4;
17
18     int permuted_array[n], inversion[n];
19     bool ready;
20     int total_inversion, i, c, sum_left_inversion;
21     i = 0;
22
23     while (i < n)
24     {
25         permuted_array[i] = i;
26         inversion[i] = 0;
27         ++i;
28     }
29
30     inversion[0] = -2;
31
32     ready = false;
33     total_inversion = 0;
34
35     while (!ready)
36     {
37         for (auto e : permuted_array)
38             std::cout << e << '\t';
39
40         std::cout << std::endl;
41
42         i = n - 1;
43         c = 0;
44         sum_left_inversion = total_inversion - inversion[i
            ];
45
46         while ((inversion[i] == i) && even(
            sum_left_inversion))
47         {
48             c = c + 1;
49             i = i - 1;
50             sum_left_inversion = sum_left_inversion -
                inversion[i];
51         }
52
53         while ((inversion[i] == 0) && odd(
            sum_left_inversion))
54         {
55             i = i - 1;
56             sum_left_inversion = sum_left_inversion -
                inversion[i];
57         }
```

```
58
59          c = c + i − inversion[i];
60
61          if (even(sum_left_inversion) && i > 0)
62          {
63              inversion[i] = inversion[i] + 1;
64              total_inversion = total_inversion + 1;
65              std::swap(permuted_array[c−1], permuted_array[c
                    ]);
66          }
67          else if(odd(sum_left_inversion) && i > 0)
68          {
69              inversion[i] = inversion[i] − 1;
70              total_inversion = total_inversion − 1;
71              std::swap(permuted_array[c], permuted_array[c +
                    1]);
72          }
73          else if(i == 0)
74          {
75              ready = true;
76          }
77      }
78 }
```

In the program given above, inversion[0], which should be constantly 0, has been assigned the funny value -2; this is the usual, mean, little coding trick, in order to let the search for the right-most changeable inversion[i] value terminate artificially when there is no more such an inversion[i] value. The value *total_inversion* records the total number of inversions in the array *permuted_array*, that is used to record the permutation; the variable *sum_left_inversion* records the sum of the (non-funny) inversion[j] values to the left of inversion[i] (i.e. with j < i).

Chapter 18

The Non-Crooks Problem

Problem 18

Array $f[0..F-1]$ contains the names of people who work at Cornell, in alphabetical order. Array $g[0..G-1]$ contains the names of people on welfare at Ithaca, in alphabetical order. Thus, neither array contains duplicates and both arrays are monotonically increasing:

$$f[0] < f[1] < f[2] < \ldots < f[F-1]$$
$$g[0] < g[1] < g[2] < \ldots < g[G-1]$$

Count the number of people who are presumably not crooks: those that appear in at least one array but not in both.

Solution

18.1 Assertion

The result assertion is

$$R : c = (i : 0 \le i < F : f[i] \notin g[0..G-1]) + (j : 0 \le j < G : g[j] \notin f[0..F-1])$$

18.2 Invariant

We would expect to write a program that sequences up the two arrays together, in some synchronized fashion, performing a count as it goes. Thus, it makes sense to develop an invariant by replacing the two constants F and G of R as follows:

$$0 \le h \le F \wedge 0 \le k \le G \wedge c = (i : 0 \le i < h : f[i] \notin g[0..G-1]) + (j : 0 \le j < k : g[j] \notin f[0..F-1])$$

18.3 Analysis

Now, consider execution of $h \leftarrow h + 1$. Under what conditions does its execution leave p true ? The condition for this command must obviously imply $f[h] \notin g[0..G-1]$, but we want the condition to be simple. As it stands, this seems out of the question.

Perhaps strengthening the invariant will allow us to find a simple job. One thing we have not tried to exploit is moving through the arrays in a synchronized fashion, the invariant does not imply this at all. Suppose we add to the invariant the conditions $f[h-1] < g[k]$ and $g[k-1] < f[h]$, this might provide the synchronized search that we desire. That is, we use the invariant

$$P : 0 \le h \le F \wedge 0 \le k \le G \wedge f[h-1] < g[k] \wedge g[k-1] < f[h]$$
$$c = (i : 0 \le i < h : f[i] \notin g[0..G-1]) + (j : 0 \le j < k : g[j] \notin f[0..F-1])$$

Then the additional condition $f[h] < g[k]$ yields

$$g[k-1] < f[h] < g[k]$$

so that $f[h]$ does not appear in G, and increasing h will maintain the invariant. Similarly the condition for $k \leftarrow k+1$ will be $g[k] < f[h]$.

18.4 Algorithm

This gives us our program, written below. We assume the existence of virtual values $f[-1] = g[i-1] = -\infty$ and $f[F] = g[G] = +\infty$; this allows us to dispense with worries about boundary conditions in the invariant.

Algorithm 44 The Non-Crooks Program

1: $h \leftarrow 0, k \leftarrow 0, c \leftarrow 0$
2: $invariant : P, bound : F - p + G - q$
3: **while** $f \ne F \wedge g \ne G$ **do**
4:      **if** $f[h] < g[k]$ **then**
5:          $h \leftarrow h + 1$
6:          $c \leftarrow c + 1$
7:      **else if** $f[h] == g[k]$ **then**
8:          $h \leftarrow h + 1$
9:          $k \leftarrow k + 1$
10:     **else if** $f[h] > g[k]$ **then**
11:         $k \leftarrow k + 1$
12:         $c \leftarrow c + 1$
13:     **end if**
14: **end while**
15: *Add to c the number of unprocessed elements of f and g:*
16: $c \leftarrow c + F - h + G - k$

Chapter 19

Median Search Problem

Problem 19

Let $X[1, \ldots, n]$ and $Y[1, \ldots, n]$ be two arrays, each containing
n numbers already in sorted order. Give an $O(\log n)$-time algorithm to find the
median of all 2n elements in arrays X and Y

Solution

19.1 Analysis

Assume that when n is even the median of X is $X[\frac{n}{2} + 1]$. If the arrays are of
equal size, and that is the current case, we can solve the problem by a divide and
conquer algorithm that compares the medians of the two arrays and then discards
the lower half of the array with the smaller median and the upper half of the array
with the bigger median. The algorithm proceeds likewise until both arrays are
reduced to 2 elements each. Then we solve the reduced problem in constant time.
In case the size is odd, by upper and lower half we mean, the subarray from one
end until and excluding the median. It is easy to show this dichotomy brings the
size of the array down to 2 regardless of what the initial n is, because the iterator
$n \leftarrow \frac{n}{2}$ reaches 2 regardless of the starting value of n.

Now consider a more general version of this problem where the arrays are $X[1, \ldots, p]$ and $Y[1, \ldots, q]$ for possibly unequal values of p and q. Let us call
Z the array that would be obtained if we merged X and Y. Let m = p + q. The
essence is the fact that we can check in $\Theta(1)$ time whether X[i] is the median of Z,
for any i such that $1 \leq i \leq p$. According to our definition of median, the median
is greater than or equal to $\lfloor m \rfloor$ elements of an m-element array. Having that in
mind, clearly if X[i] is the median then:

- X[i] is greater than or equal to i - 1 elements of X.

- X[i] is greater than or equal to $j = \lfloor m \rfloor - i + 1$ elements of Y.

It takes only constant time to check if $Y[j] \leq X[i] \leq Y[j + 1]$. To avoid excessive
boundary checks, pad X and Y at the left side with $-\infty$ and with $+\infty$ at the right
side. If that is fulfilled we have found the median and it is X[i]. Otherwise, we
binary search in X to see if the median is in X. If that fails, the median must be
from Y, and we can repeat the analogous process with X and Y swapped.

19.2 Algorithm

Algorithm 45 Find Median of two sorted array

1: **function** COMMON-MEDIAN(X[1,..., p], Y[1,..., q]) ▷ sorted arrays
2:    $m \leftarrow p + q$
3:    $k \leftarrow$ MEDIAN-BIN-SEARCH$(X, Y, 1, p)$
4:    **if** k > 0 **then**
5:        **return** X, k
6:    **end if**
7:    $k \leftarrow$ MEDIAN-BIN-SEARCH$(Y, X, 1, q)$
8:    **return** Y, k
9: **end function**

Algorithm 46 Median Search

1: **function** MEDIAN-BIN-SEARCH(A, B: sorted arrays, l, r:integers)
2:    **if** l > r **then**
3:        **return** -1
4:    **end if**
5:    $i \leftarrow \lfloor \frac{l+r}{2} \rfloor$
6:    $j \leftarrow \lfloor \frac{m}{2} \rfloor - i + 1$
7:    **if** $B[j] \leq A[i] \leq B[j+1]$ **then**
8:        **return** i
9:    **end if**
10:   **if** $A[i] < B[j]$ **then**
11:       MEDIAN-BIN-SEARCH(A, B, l, i)
12:   **end if**
13:   **if** $A[i] > B[j+1]$ **then**
14:       MEDIAN-BIN-SEARCH(A, B, i + 1, r)
15:   **end if**
16: **end function**

A not too formal proof of correctness of COMMON-MEDIAN is simply pointing out the preceding discussion and knowing that the binary search idea is correct. The time complexity is obviously $\Theta(\log m)$. Alternatively, we can say the complexity is $\Theta(max\{\log p, \log q\})$.

Chapter 20

Missing Integer Problem

Problem 20

An array A[1, . . . , n] contains all the integers from 0 to n except one. It would be easy to determine the missing integer in $O(n)$ time by using an auxiliary array B[0, . . . , n] to record which numbers appear in A. In this problem, however, we cannot access an entire integer in A with a single operation. The elements of A are represented in binary, and the only operation we can use to access them is fetch the jth bit of A[i], which takes constant time. Show that if we use only this operation, we can still determine the missing integer in $O(n)$ time.

Solution

20.1 Analysis

Let m be the number of bits required to represent n in binary. It is well known that $m = \lfloor \log_2 n \rfloor + 1$. In this problem we think of A as an $m \times n$, 0-1 matrix. Row number m of A consists of the least significant bits of the numbers in A, row number m 1 consists of the second least significant bits, etc., row number 1 consists of the most significant bits.

For instance, if n = 10 and the missing number is $6 = 0110_b$, A may look like:

Printing this array in spiral form would give

$$1\ 2\ 3\ 4\ 8\ 12\ 16\ 15\ 14\ 13\ 9\ 5\ 6\ 7\ 11\ 10$$

The only constant time access to it is of the form A[j][i], which can be labeled as *fetch the jth bit of A[i]*, assuming the first bit is the most significant, etc.

20.2 C++ Implementation

Consider the following program:

```
1  int m = floor (logb(n)) + 1;
2  int A[m][n];
3
4  int main ()
5  {
6      int i, j, t, numrow, n0, n1, ntemp = n;
7      int B[n], res[m];
8
9      for (i = 0; i < n; i ++)
10     {
11         B[i] = i;
12     }
13
14     for (i = m - 1; i >= 0; i --)
15     {
16         n0 = n1 = 0;
17
18         for (j = 0; j < ntemp; j ++)
19         {
20             if (A[i][B[j]] == 0) n0 ++;
21             else n1 ++;
22         }
23
24         if (n0 - n1 == 2 || n0 - n1 = 1) res[i] = 1;
25         if (n0 - n1 == 0 || n0 - n1 == -1) res[i] = 0;
26
27         for (j = 0, t = 0; j < ntemp; j ++)
28         {
29             if ((res[i] == A[i][B[j]]))
30             {
31                 B[t] = B[j];
32                 t ++;
33             }
34         }
35
36         if (ntemp \% 2 == 0) ntemp = (ntemp / 2);
37         else if (res[i] == 0) ntemp = floor (ntemp / 2);
38         else ntemp = ceil (ntemp / 2);
39     }
40
41     for (i = 0; i < n; i ++)
42     std :: cout <<   res[i]);
43  }
```

We claim the algorithm implemented by this program solves correctly the problem of determining the missing bit. First we prove it is correct.

20.3 Proving the Correctness of the program

Define that a complete array of size n is a two dimensional bit array similar to the above A but without any missing column from it. Clearly, such an array has n + 1 columns. For instance, a complete array of size 10 would be the following:

Define that an almost complete array of size n is a two dimensional bit array with precisely one missing column from it. It follows the array A in the current problem is an almost complete array of size n. Now consider any complete array $\tilde{A}$ of size n. Call $\tilde{L}$ the bottom row of $\tilde{A}$. That $\tilde{L}$ consists of the least significant bits of the numbers from $\tilde{A}$. Let $\tilde{n}_0$ be the number of zeros and $\tilde{n}_1$, the number of ones, in $\tilde{L}$. Let $\tilde{\Delta} = \tilde{n}_0 - \tilde{n}_1$. We claim that :

$$\tilde{\Delta} = \begin{cases} 0, & \text{if } n \text{ is odd.} \\ 1, & \text{if } n \text{ is even..} \end{cases} \tag{20.1}$$

Indeed, it is trivial to prove by induction that if the number n + 1 of columns in $\tilde{A}$ is even then $\tilde{\Delta} = 0$ and if it is odd, $\tilde{A} = 1$.

Now consider A: any almost complete array of size n, obtained from $\tilde{A}$ by deleting a column, i.e., the missing number. Let L be the bottom row of A. Let n_0 be the number of zeros and n_1 , the number of ones, in L. Let $\Delta = n_0 - n_1$. We claim that:

$$\Delta = \begin{cases} \tilde{\Delta} + 1, & \text{if the missing number is odd.} \\ \tilde{\Delta} - 1, & \text{if the missing number is even.} \end{cases} \tag{20.2}$$

Indeed, if the missing number is even there is a 0 less in L in comparison with $\tilde{L}$, while the number of ones is the same; that is, $n_0 = \tilde{n}_0 - 1$ and $n_1 = \tilde{n}_1$. Likewise, if the missing number is odd there is a 1 less in L in comparison with $\tilde{L}$, while the number of zeros is the same; that is, $n_0 = \tilde{n}_0$ and $n_1 = \tilde{n}_1 - 1$. Having in mind the above considerations, it is clear that:

$$\Delta = \begin{cases} 2, & \text{if } n \text{ is even and the missing number is odd.} \\ 1, & \text{if } n \text{ is odd and the missing number is odd.} \\ 0, & \text{if } n \text{ is even and the missing number is even.} \\ -1, & \text{if } n \text{ is odd and the missing number is even.} \end{cases} \tag{20.3}$$

We conclude that :

$\Delta \in \{1, 2\} \implies$ the least significant bit of the missing number is 1.
$\Delta \in \{-1, 0\} \implies$ the least significant bit of the missing number is 0.

So, with one linear scan along the bottom row of A we can compute Δ and then in constant time we can compute the least significant bit of the missing number. However, if we attempt a similar approach for the other bits of the missing number, we will end up with $\Omega(n \log n)$ computation because the number of rows is logarithmic in n. The key observation is that in order to determine the second least significant bit of the missing number, we need to scan approximately half the columns of A. Namely, if the least significant bit was determined to be 1, for the computation of the second least significant bit we need to scan only the columns having 1 at the bottom row. Likewise, if the least significant bit was determined to be 0, for the computation of the second least significant bit we need to scan only the columns having 0 at the bottom row. Next we explain why this is true.

The number of rows of A is $m = \lfloor \log_2 n \rfloor + 1$. Define that $A_0^{(m-1)}$ is the two dimensional array obtained from A by deleting the columns that have 0 in row m - 1, and then deleting row m - 1. Define that $A_1^{(m-1)}$ is the two dimensional array obtained from A by deleting the columns that have 1 in row m - 1, and then deleting row m - 1. Call the process of deriving $A_0^{(m-1)}$ and $A_1^{(m-1)}$, the *reduction* of A, and the two obtained arrays, the *reduced arrays*. Let b be the least significant bit of the missing number and $\bar{b}$ be its complement.

20.3.1   Lemma

Under the current naming conventions, $A_b^{(m-1)}$ is complete, and $A_{\bar{b}}^{(m-1)}$ is almost complete. Furthermore, the missing number in $A_{\bar{b}}^{(m-1)}$ is obtained from the missing number in A by removing the least significant bit (i.e., shift right).

20.3.2   Proof

First we will see an example and then make a formal proof. To use the previously given example with n = 10, m = 4, missing number $6 = 0110_b$, and A as

the two derived subarrays : $A_0^{(3)}$ and $A_1^{(3)}$ are respectively:

Obviously, $A_0^{(3)}$ is complete and $A_1^{(3)}$ is almost complete: column $\{0\ 1\ 1\}$ is missing from it. The least significant bit of the missing number in A is 0; if we did not know which is the missing number, we could deduce that its least significant bit is 0 by computing the aforementioned $\Delta = 5 - 5 = 0$. Indeed $A_{\tilde{0}}^{(3)} = A_1^{(3)}$ is the array that is almost complete. And indeed the missing number in it 011 is obtained from 0110 by shift right.

Let us prove it. It is clear that if $\tilde{A}$ is a complete array of size n, both $A_0^{(\tilde{m}-1)}$ and $A_1^{(\tilde{m}-1)}$ are complete. If n is odd then they contain the same columns (possibly in different order left to right), otherwise $A_1^{(\tilde{m}-1)}$ contains one column more and the other columns are the same. Now imagine A; the array obtained from $\tilde{A}$ by the deletion of precisely one column. If the bit at the bottom row of the deleted column is 0 then $A_0^{(m-1)}$ is the same as $A_0^{(\tilde{m}-1)}$, so $A_0(m-1)$ is complete. However, $A_1^{(m-1)}$ is not the same as $A_1^{(\tilde{m}-1)}$: $A_1^{(\tilde{m}-1)}$ contains one more column that corresponds to the missing number. It follows that $A_1^{(m-1)}$ is almost complete. Alternatively, if the bit at the bottom row of the deleted column is 1 then $A_1^{(m-1)}$ is the same as $A_1^{(\tilde{m}-1)}$, so $A_1^{(m-1)}$ is complete, but $A_0^{(m-1)}$ is almost complete. ■

Verification of the algorithm

Having all that in mind, the verification of the algorithm is straightforward. m is the number of bits, i.e. the number of rows of A. The array res is the output: at each iteration of the main for loop, one bit of res is computed, the direction being from the least significant bit *upwards*. B is an auxilliary array of integers. The definition of the problem requires bitwise access only to the elements of A; the array B can be accessed *normally*. B keeps the indices of the columns whose i^{th} row we scan at every iteration of the main for loop.

Initially, of course, B contains the indices 0, 1, . . . , n-1, in that order, so when i is m-1 we simply scan the bottom row of A. At every iteration of the main for loop, ntemp is the number of columns in the almost complete array whose last row we scan. Initially, ntemp is n, which reflects the fact that at the first iteration we scan the bottom row of A. We will verify the assignment of new value to ntemp later on.

Within the main for loop, the first nested for loop simply counts the zeros and ones and stores the results in n0 and n1, respectively.

The difference n0 - n1 determines the ith least significant bit res[i] according to the following

$$\Delta \in \{1, 2\} \implies \text{ the least significant bit of the missing number is 1.}$$
$$\Delta \in \{-1, 0\} \implies \text{ the least significant bit of the missing number is 0.}$$

The second nested for loop discovers the indices of the columns that correspond to the columns of the next reduced array that is almost complete. To see why we consider only values (of the last row of A) equal to res[i], check the above Lemma.

Finally, the assignment of new value to ntemp is done in accordance to the following considerations. If ntemp is even then both derived arrays have the same length $\frac{ntemp}{2}$. Otherwise, note that we are interested in that derived subarray that is almost complete. If res[i] is one then that subarray is the one obtained by deleting the columns with zeros at the bottom; it has one more column than the complete derived subarray, so res[i] should be $ceil(\frac{ntemp}{2})$. Analogously, if res[i] is zero then res[i] should be $floor(\frac{ntemp}{2})$. That concludes the verification of the algorithm. The reader is invited to make an even more rigorous proof of correctness using *loop invariant*.

The number of accesses to A at each iteration of the main for loop is proportional to the current value of ntemp. Clearly, the total number of accesses is proportional to

$$n + \frac{n}{2} + \frac{n}{4} + \ldots + 1 \leq 2n = \Theta(n)$$

Bibliography

[1] G.J.E. Rawlins, *Compared to what ? An introduction to the analysis of algorithms*. Computer Science Press, 1992.

[2] N. Alon, M. Blum, A. Fiat, S. Kannan, M. Naor, and R. Ostrovsky, *Matching Nuts and Bolts*. Proceedings of the 5th Annual Symposium on Discrete Algorithms, ACM- SIAM Press, 690-696, 1994.

[3] Phillip G. Bradford, *Matching Nuts and Bolts Optimally*. 1995.

[4] David Gries, *The Science of Programming(Monographs in Computer Science)*. Springer (February 1, 1987).

[5] Boost C++ Libraries @*http://www.boost.org*

[6] http://community.topcoder.com/tc?module=Static &d1=tutorials&d2=lowestCommonAncestor

[7] Leslie Lamport, *LATEX: A Document Preparation System*. Addison Wesley, Massachusetts, 2nd Edition, 1994.

Index

Index